A Joyful Passion for Teaching

A Joyful Passion for Teaching

Edited by

Al Stramiello, Ed.D.
Mary Willingham, Ed.D.
Carl Martray, Ph.D.

MERCER UNIVERSITY PRESS
Macon, Georgia
2006

ISBN 0-86554-/997-4

MUP/P344

© 2006 Mercer University Press
1400 Coleman Road
Macon, Georgia 31207

First Edition.

The paper used in this publication meets the minimum
requirements of American National Standard for Information
Sciences—Permanence of Paper for Printed Library Materials,
ANSI Z39.48-1984.

Library of Congress Cataloging-in-Publication Data

A joyful passion for teaching / edited by Al Stramiello, Mary Willingham
and
Carl Martray.
    p. cm.
Includes bibliographical references and index.
ISBN-13: 978-0-86554-997-5 (pbk. : alk. paper)
ISBN-10: 0-86554-997-4 (pbk. : alk. paper)
1. Teachers—United States—Anecdotes. 2. Teaching—United
States—Anecdotes. I. Stramiello, Al. II. Willingham, Mary. III. Martray,
Carl.

LB1775.2.J69 2006
371.1—dc22

                                            2006001479

In memory of

Alicia Anne Stramiello

1984–2004

Acknowledgements

For our students, may you always carry forth our joyful passion for teaching.

The editors are especially grateful to the Book Review Advisory Committee. Their collaboration and commitment were without waiver. The members of the committee included the following: Mary Kay Bacallao, Ed.D.; Jacquelyn Culpepper, Ph.D.; Carolyn Garvin, Professor; H. Anne Hathaway, Ed.D.; Susan C. Malone, Ed.D.; and Emilie Warner Paille, Ed.D.

Contents

Introduction

Carl R. Martray, Ph.D.
Dean, Tift College of Education

Dedication, compassion, and commitment are common threads that weave their way through the pages of *A Joyful Passion for Teaching*, which is composed of a series of essays expressing individual, yet common, themes of reflection upon the teaching experience. It is my honor and pleasure to welcome you to this book and to make a few comments concerning its contents and the goal of the faculty of Tift College of Education at Mercer University who contributed to its development. I believe that as you read the personal expressions communicated by the individuals comprising the faculty who contributed to this book, you will gain insight as to their passion for teaching and the common beliefs that bring them together as a faculty with a common bond.

The faculty of Tift College of Education has stated openly a common set of values in the form of a conceptual framework, which serves as the underlying foundation for its programs. The framework, "The Transforming Practitioner," reflects the beliefs of the faculty and serves as the theme upon which its programs are developed. The following definition and brief description of the conceptual framework will provide you with the foundation upon which our faculty operates and our programs are developed.

Definition of "The Transforming Practitioner"

"The Transforming Practitioner," a living link in the educational process, is an educator who is changing internally through understanding, practicing, and reflecting such that, individually and collaboratively, he or she implements for all learners appropriate and significant life-changing experiences that effectively provide for the needs of the individual, actively engage students in the learning process, and promote life-long learning.

The Conceptual Framework

Within the context of a distinctive Baptist heritage, the inclusion of the Paideia ideal, the know-how of blending theory and practice, Tift College of Education has chosen the *To Know, To Do, and To Be* principles as the Conceptual Framework that undergirds its teacher education and educational leadership programs at Mercer University.

The Conceptual Framework, *To Know, To Do, To Be*, prepares the candidate to adapt and meet the needs of a current and changing society while highlighting the Baptist tradition of promoting mediation, settlement, compromise, and understanding in the classroom, in the school system, and in the community. Preparing the candidate to be a Transforming Practitioner is vital to successful educational practice in increasingly diverse settings. Blending theory with field experiences helps to actualize this preparation both for teachers and educational leaders.

Teachers and educational leaders who are Transforming Practitioners must embrace the processes of *understanding, practicing,* and *reflecting,* which are indeed vital components of transformation. Each of these three processes is important and meaningful in itself, but the three are also interconnected in very real ways. Understanding informs practice. The wisdom developed through practice increases and modified understanding and, ideally, leads to rich and meaningful reflection. Reflection causes teachers and educational leaders to enhance their levels of understanding and to make substantive as well as subtle changes in their practice. These processes of understanding, practicing, and reflecting are themes that are infused in and richly woven throughout the principles of the Conceptual Framework: To Know, To Do, and To Be.

Discussions among faculty pertaining to the philosophical bases upon which our programs are developed facilitated the realization of the fact that we actively and purposefully share our beliefs as a unit through reviewing and educating our students in our conceptual framework. These discussions also led to the realization that although we engage our students in discussion concerning our conceptual framework, we as a faculty have not made a concerted effort to communicate and share our personal stories, thoughts, strategies, and philosophies with our students. In discussions concerning this issue, our faculty could not identify an instance in which they as a group attempted to communicate these ideas with the students with whom they interact and prepare as professional educators. Thus, the faculty of Tift College of Education decided to engage in a collaborative effort designed to communicate personal thoughts and examples as to how they continually strive to model "The Transforming Practitioner" ideals in their practice. Sharing our passion for teaching and what drives us as educators with our students and other professionals, as well as those considering the profession, became a common goal for this book as discussion progressed.

As you read through the essays in this book, you will find clear expressions of passion for the practice of teaching as well as commitment of faculty to work together with our students to strive for the ideals characterized by the "Transforming Practitioner" concept. We are pleased you have chosen to read *A Joyful Passion for Teaching* and you have interest in the profession that we embrace.

First-Graders, Apple Memories, and Monsters

Mary E. Willingham, Ed.D.

"This is a big bunch of crap! Whadda we have to know this stuff for?" And still another student chimed in, "So what?" These were the comments of my ninth-grade students, and they were said to me many years ago when I was a very green novice, only a few months into my first teaching job. This group of struggling readers truly believed that whatever it was I was asking them to read or do made about as much sense as if I had asked them to translate Homer's *Odyssey* from the ancient Greek. Reading, learning, and school in general were totally irrelevant to their lives. On this they all agreed. Refusing to have a complete meltdown so early into my brand new career, I took their comments home and pondered over them. In fact, I spent the rest of that first year pondering over these unruly students and my sad fate to have been assigned, as new teachers generally are, to such an undisciplined and undesirable lot.

From that very first year, however, I knew two things. First, my teacher training had not prepared me to deal with these students, and second, I knew even from that very first day that these students could learn. I had seen them in their part-time jobs after school, and I had watched them take on many adult responsibilities for their siblings. They were poor, by and large. They hated school. But they were not stupid, even though many of their more affluent peers and teachers thought so and told them so on a regular basis.

So I spent that year and the next couple of years trying to teach these students and, all the while, thinking about why they seemed so difficult to educate. When I had a thought or read an article or book that seemed to shed light on this problem, I got out my journal and wrote down whatever had occurred to me. At the time, I never dreamed that these thoughts would become the heart of my future teaching and lectures.

One thought that occurred to me early on seemed so obvious that I wondered why no one had ever mentioned it. I was thinking particularly of my public school colleagues, and especially my teacher-education professors. This thought and observation had two parts:

> (Part 1) Virtually 100 percent of first-grade children want (indeed, are desperate) to learn to read.
>
> (Part 2) I was spending everyday trying to teach a class of hostile and unmotivated adolescents who would rather be anywhere than in a schoolroom learning.

I asked myself, "Am I missing something here, or is this really the huge disconnect that it seemed?" What happened to all that marvelous motivation in the years between first grade and high school (or, as a colleague pointed out, between first grade and third grade)? So this was my first observation.

I also wrote in my journal about salted apples. At least that is how this important memory came to me. In the school cafeteria one day at lunch during those first years of teaching, I accidentally salted my fruit salad. When I took a bite of apple and salt, I had a Madeleine cake moment of which Proust would have been proud. My salted apple took me back to the evenings spent listening to my mother read to me. My father traveled and was gone most of the week, so many weeknights I would climb in bed next to my mother and watch while she pealed, cored, sprinkled salt on an apple, gave me half, and began to read aloud. We read all the classics that way. I became a horse lover in *Black Beauty*, a life-long mountain hiker in *Heidi*, a lover of tree houses and efficiency in *A Swiss Family Robinson*, a passionate gardener from *A Secret Garden*, and a lover of animals (especially dogs) from *Watch* and *White Fang*. As I thought back to those bedtimes reading with my mother, I was struck by one particular aspect of the experience; my mother loved these stories as much as I did. And I now know why that was. My grandmother died when my mother was very young, and in the ensuing years, no one ever read to her. These stories were as fresh and new for her as they were for me. This gave a power and reality to those moments that they might not have had under other circumstances. We, both of us, wept and laughed with joy as we read our way through these timeless books.

My third epiphany also occurred sometime during that first or second year of teaching. My school was near Washington, DC, and one weekend my husband and I went to see the Holocaust Museum. It was an unforgettable experience. So powerful were the images left in one's mind and soul that I thought a visit to this particular museum should be a pilgrimage for everyone. As I was talking about this to my cousin's husband, he told me that all of his father's family had perished in the Holocaust and to see the horrors catalogued there would simply be too excruciatingly painful. It was shortly after that conversation that I read Haim Ginott's cautionary statement:

> Dear Teacher:
> I am a survivor of a concentration camp. My eyes saw what no man should witness: gas chambers built by learned engineers; children poisoned by educated physicians; infants killed by trained nurses; women and babies shot and burned by high school and college graduates. So I am suspicious of education.
>
> My request is: help your students become more human. Your efforts must never produce learned monsters, skilled psychopaths, educated Eichmanns.
>
> Reading, writing, and arithmetic are important only if they serve to make our children more humane.[1]

During these early years of my career, I wrote down many thoughts and anecdotes and recorded ideas from numerous books and articles, but when I think of the origins of my joyful passion for teaching, it is to these three

---

[1] Haim G. Ginott, *Teacher and Child: A Book for Parents and Teachers* (New York: Scribner, 1993) 317.

memories that I return. I find that they continue to give me insight, guidance, and energy.

Each one of these three observations and experiences from the past has as its central element a command for all teachers: Minds and souls are to be handled judiciously (first-graders and their priceless motivation); encouraged with authenticity (salt, apples, and real tears); and opened to wisdom and goodness (the truly educated celebrate life and not evil).

The child that enters first grade has all the motivation necessary to ask all the important questions and learn all about the magnificent and fragile world and the people who live upon it. All this child needs is a joyful and passionate teacher.

For Bobby Hargason...Wherever He Is

Al Stramiello, Ed.D.

The year was 1955. The Cold War between the United States and Russia continued to escalate with ever increasing tensions between the two countries. General Eisenhower had been elected president with running mate Richard M. Nixon, who would later become infamous. In Montgomery, Alabama, Rosa Parks refused to take a seat at the back of the bus. The Brooklyn Dodgers beat the New York Yankees in the World Series. Turmoil was evident throughout the world. But, in the quiet rural borough of White Oak, Pennsylvania, life was tranquil for the students attending Lincoln Elementary School. It was especially peaceful and predictable for me. I was in the second grade. Mrs. Hall led our class through the academic intricacies of phonics, memorizing math facts, and learning about various cloud formations. The last Friday of every month brought the Peterson Handwriting System Man to our school. I don't remember him having a real name. I remember his plain gray suit with a white shirt—buttons on the collar were not yet fashionable—and charcoal tie. I especially remember his shoes. They were black and always scuffed. He would tower over us second-graders as we labored intensively on forming the letters in perfect cursive script. The Peterson Man never smiled. I don't think he was allowed to smile. His was a look of consternation as he walked deliberately up and down the second-grade aisles. I distinctly remember thinking that the Peterson Man's look of intensity was a sign of the importance of learning perfect penmanship. His was a job of great importance, supervising America's second-graders in their quest for perfect penmanship. It wasn't until later in life that it struck me that he probably viewed his job as being utterly boring.

It was as though Lincoln Elementary School was a scene etched in Norman Rockwell's imagination. The school was a two-story structure with long ivy vines lazily winding their way up the warm, earth-tone bricks. It was nestled cozily in a peaceful neighborhood with asphalt paved drives and one story houses. Lincoln Elementary could have been a magnet with all the surrounding houses drawn close around it. Local elementary student lore had it that the principal of the school had an electric paddling machine in his office. I could only imagine how the contraption might have worked. In my mind it probably looked like a Rube Goldberg invention with a high wood back and straight slats for arms. Surely, there had to be wires coming out from the two paddles that noncompliant third-graders had to sit on. The wires must have been heavy and black, the better to carry the electric current. They went straight into the electrical outlet on the wall behind the chair. Thinking back on it, I don't remember ever meeting an eyewitness who had actually spent time strapped into the electric paddling machine. But I knew it was there. All I had to do was ask a third-grader. A worldly third-grader could describe it in perfect detail for any of us second-graders.

Beyond Lincoln Elementary School's playground stood a monument to the Duncan Yo-Yo. There, clearly visible from my second-grade classroom windows, stood Swanson's Candy Store. Old man Swanson and his wife sold candy and other mouth-watering treats that would whet the appetite of any student who had spent the day slaving away at arithmetic worksheets and memorizing the capitols of the forty-eight states. Every kid at Lincoln School knew that the melting of winter and the coming of spring meant just one thing. The Duncan Yo-Yo man was coming to town! But not just to town. It was much bigger than that. He was coming to Swanson's Candy Store to demonstrate his latest yo-yo tricks. Oh, if only I could learn to "walk the dog" or swing my yo-yo "around the world." He always timed his visits for 3:00 in the afternoon. It was the precise time that the dismissal bell would ring at Lincoln School. We would race across the playground in great anticipation of getting as close as possible to the king of the yo-yo. He may have had a name but formalities didn't matter. He was "the" Duncan Yo-yo man. Of course, there may have been dozens like him visiting candy stores all across the country. But this was different. He was our own Duncan Yo-yo man. Every time he visited, yo-yo sales would skyrocket at Swanson's Candy Store.

Life began to change for me in the spring of second grade. It wouldn't be until years later that I would begin to understand how significant that change would be. Just down the street from Swanson's Candy Store, several houses away, stood a small red brick home. Its narrow front porch was surrounded by a green iron railing with a gate. Blue Spruce trees towered in front of the house. While sitting at my desk, over in the first row beside the windows, I could sometimes faintly see a small figure playing on the porch. There wasn't much to see; just an outline of what I thought might be a boy. During the first several months of school, I didn't pay much attention to the figure on the porch. Actually, I really never thought much about who might be over there in the house down from Swanson's.

Recess was an important part of life at Lincoln Elementary School. It was much more than an important part of life. Recess was what every self-respecting second-grade boy lived for. Walking somberly down the hall in a straight line with Mrs. Hall in the lead would always be followed by an explosive burst of energy as we blasted out the door and onto the playground. While most of the playground was hard, black asphalt, the part that was especially enticing lay out at the far reaches of the schoolyard. Way, way out there lay the grass field that became our special place for wild, fun filled games of dodgeball, football, and our own special game called "everybody tackle the guy with the ball."

Life changed the day a mother and her son stepped off the front of the red brick house's porch to walk across Lincoln School's playground. At first I didn't pay much attention to them. I was too busy trying to hold on to the football while everybody dragged me down to the ground in a heap. But then I heard a woman's voice talking to us. It wasn't Mrs. Hall talking. This was a sad voice filled with hopeful expectations. She said her name was Mrs. Hargason. The faint silhouette that I sometimes saw playing on the porch was Bobby Hargason, her son. He was much bigger than my second-grade friends; bigger even than the Walter twins, Sammy and Jimmy. His hair was blond and looked unkempt. His eyes were kind of squinted even though the sun wasn't glaring at him. We could hardly understand whatever it was that he said to us. His speech was a little too hard to understand. But it didn't matter. It was Mrs. Hargason who did all of the talking. "Can Bobby play with you boys at recess? He doesn't have any friends."

We didn't ask any questions. I don't remember any of us asking questions. We just knew that here was a kid who was just enough bigger than us, and harmless looking enough, that we could give him the football and tackle him. We didn't tackle him in a harmful way. The pure fun of it was that Bobby Hargason loved trying to run with the football while a group of us second-graders dragged him to the ground by his pants legs. He would mumble and laugh and squeal, seemingly, all at the same time. But then the recess bell would ring again, and we second-graders would dust ourselves off and trudge back into the classroom. Playing with Bobby Hargason became an almost daily ritual. His mom would watch for Mrs. Hall's class to come out the side door, and she would then take her son's hand and walk across the lot to the grass field. No matter what the game, Bobby became a part of our recess.

The funny thing was though, that Bobby Hargason would never trudge into the classroom with us. To this day, almost fifty years later, I can still see Bobby Hargason holding his mother's hand and walking across the schoolyard...away from Lincoln School. As I would wipe the sweat off my forehead and briskly shake the dirt from the folds in my double cuffed jeans, I would watch as they walked home and wonder why I had to go back into the classroom while Bobby Hargason went home. Life didn't seem fair to a second-grader. Why was it that I had to go back into Lincoln

Elementary School for more Peterson Handwriting lessons and math and reading, but Bobby Hargason got to go home?

It wasn't until many years later that the lesson of Bobby Hargason was learned. The injustice wasn't that my second-grade classmates and I had to study math and reading while Bobby Hargason got to spend the day playing on his front porch and watching television. The real injustice was that Bobby Hargason and thousands of other children with disabilities did not have the same opportunities as I did. Having a disability meant that you could be denied access to the public school system. It wasn't until almost twenty years later that the injustice was corrected with the passing of Public Law 94–142, The Education for All Handicapped Children Act.

As the years went on I would sometimes think back to Bobby Hargason. Even though Bobby was mentally retarded, his existence taught me one of the most meaningful lessons that I have learned in life. The true lesson of Bobby Hargason is that I was put on Earth to serve. Deep in my soul I understand that, for me, the real purpose of my life is to help others, especially those with disabilities. My wife and I have been involved with special education students since we entered college in the mid-1960s. All of our college degrees are in special education. We both understand the importance of valuing those with disabilities and realizing the importance they can make as they become contributing members of society.

My joy-filled passion for teaching rests fully in the area of special education. While others may find it rewarding to work with general education students or with those who are gifted, the greatest reward for me is to take a child who has been targeted by his or her teachers as being an academic failure, a child who can't learn, and teaching that child that he or she can be a success. Give me a kid who is behind the eight ball, academically, any day. Those are the students whom I love to teach. There is something so very rewarding about watching a child who thinks he can't succeed and then helping him learn. As time has gone on I also came to the realization that I could have an even greater impact by helping future teachers realize the importance of their impact upon the disabled. Thus, my teaching at the university level has reached a high level of personal significance in knowing that by shaping and molding the attitudes of regular educators my impact can have long lasting effects.

There are certain guiding principles that I hold forth as a teacher, whether it is tutoring students with significant learning disabilities or teaching at the university level. While some of these principles are theoretically based, others have been developed through my own personal experiences, both as a teacher as well as a student. One of the most important guiding principles was taught to me by my first-grade teacher, Mrs. Howinger. It was my first year of school. In those days there were no kindergarten classes at Lincoln Elementary. Mrs. Howinger was a short lady. Even with her high heels on, she seemed just a little taller than the students in her class. Her glasses were thick and gently slid down to almost the tip of her nose. Her wrinkled cheeks were always covered with an ample amount of heavy red rouge.

Lincoln Elementary always held a parent's night during the first month of school. Moms and dads would first assemble in a large group in the auditorium where the principal would discuss the upcoming events of the year. The best part of the evening was when parents were sent to their children's classroom. The hallways were filled with samples of the students' work and gaily decorated class doors awaited them. It was with those hall decorations in mind that Mrs. Howinger handed out the blue mimeographed drawings of clowns. As we opened our crayon boxes, she carefully instructed us to color the clowns as beautifully as we could. She was going to decorate the first-grade hallway with our clown pictures. The excitement of coloring those clown pictures is still etched in my memory. Every first-grader knew that one of the essentials of coloring was *always* to stay in the lines.

And so it was, with all of the intensity that I could muster, including my tongue sticking ever so slightly out my mouth, that I began the arduous task of coloring my clown. I hadn't seen any of my fellow first-graders' colorings, but I was absolutely certain that I had to be one of the best colorers in the room. I may not have been the best reader in the class, but, if there was one thing that I knew I could do well, it was color with my crayons. I remember the clown drawing as if it were yesterday. The room was silent except for the sound of crayons rubbing against paper on the hardwood desks. Mrs. Howinger soon began to inspect each first-grader's work quietly and deliberately. As we worked on the clowns, she walked slowly down the first aisle near the windows. She would stop at each student's desk and nod her head in approval. I couldn't wait for her to see my clown. I was certain that she would lavish my effort with great praise. Then she was over at the second aisle. Again, stopping at each desk to look over the student's work and offer a word of approval. Oh, the anticipation, the glory that I was about to receive when she saw my clown! There she was at the third aisle and then the fourth. My aisle was next. I worked harder and even more intensely on my clown as she rounded the back of my aisle. Then it happened! The unspeakable dread! As I was coloring my clown's oversized shoes, my red crayon slipped. Oh, no! I went out of the line! There it was. A short red crayon mark invading the empty white space beside the clown's shoe. Mrs. Howinger drew closer. My heart pounded. My pulse raced. The disappointment could not have been greater. I wanted so much for Mrs. Howinger to admire my work.

As she came up the end of my row, I quickly weighed my options. Should I try to color over the red mark with a white crayon to disguise it? Or, should I just let that awful red mark stay there for Mrs. Howinger to see? Unfortunately, my choice was the worst of all. As she drew ever closer I quietly slid my wrist over the red mark. There was no way that I was going to allow that red mark to interfere with Mrs. Howinger's words of approval. Then, she was there, right beside me. I never looked up. I could smell the perfume of her presence. Then her hand reached down to mine. Her fingers lifted the cuff of my long sleeved, corduroy shirt, and my whole arm was pulled away from the clown. There it was in plain sight. She never said a word, but her intent was clear. She wanted me to know that she had caught my mistake. There were no words of praise or approval. She dropped my hand and moved on to the student in front of me.

The ironic part of the story is that Mrs. Howinger probably forgot all about my clown coloring by the time she went to lunch that noon. During my first year of teaching special education children, I remembered Mrs. Howinger and my clown. One of my guiding principles of teaching became "Catch a kid doing something right!" Catching kids making mistakes is easy. They make mistakes all of the time. As a matter of fact, if you are a parent reading this chapter, you can probably take a brief pause and immediately think of something that your child is doing wrong. Making mistakes is an important part of the learning process. Most teachers could easily spend all of the school day catching their students doing something wrong. The catching them doing something right part is the important lesson. Helping students feel validated and worthy, whether they are at the elementary level or in the university classroom, is an integral part of successful teaching.

A second important guiding principle was taught by my high school chemistry teacher, Mr. Forter. Being the fourth of five Stramiello children was no easy task. My older sisters and brothers were successful students in school and left highly favorable impressions on their teachers, especially Coach Forter. Coach Forter was an older gentleman who also served as the coach of our high school's baseball team. His eccentricities were numerous and legendary. While always wearing a suit wasn't anything unusual for male teachers in the 1960s, it was uncommon to wear your baseball cleats and baseball cap along with your suit; especially while teaching chemistry to a class of high school sophomores. To make matters worse, Mr. Forter and I shared an unfortunate commonality. We both had the same first name, Albert. My lack of understanding of even the most basic of chemistry skills became readily apparent to Coach Forter.

It was sometime during the first six-week period of tenth grade that Coach Forter introduced the class to the procedure of balancing chemical equations. After a cursory introduction to the steps, he would call of each to the chalkboard to balance an equation in front of the class. Being a sixteen-year-old high school student, my one and only goal in life was to blend in with the rest of my sophomore class. I wasn't interested in being either the president of my class or the star quarterback of the football team. All I wanted to do was fit in. I never had any desire to attract any attention to myself, be it good or bad. Just getting along and being accepted was my main mission in high school. Coach Forter obviously had other plans for me.

There Coach Forter stood, over by the last row right beside the windows with his baseball cap, dark suit and baseball cleats. He would fold his arms and cock back his head as he clicked his cleats on the tile floor. "Albert! Albert Stramiello! Go to the board, boy! Balance this equation for the class."

Coach Forter might as well have been asking me the formula for building an atom bomb. As I clumsily wrote the wrong answer on the board, he would bellow aloud, "Albert! Albert, Albert, Albert. Albert Schweitzer. Albert Einstein. Albert Forter. Albert Stramiello. Jesus Christ, you're a disgrace to the name. Sit down boy!" The class laughed loudly as I sheepishly walked to my seat.

About a week later Coach Forter repeated the ritual. I dreaded my name being called but he was relentless. "Albert! Albert Stramiello! Go to the board, boy! Balance this equation for the class." Again, I failed miserably at the task. And again, Coach Forter would repeat, "Albert! Albert, Albert, Albert. Albert Schweitzer. Albert Einstein. Albert Forter. Albert Stramiello. Jesus Christ, you're a disgrace to the name. Sit down boy!" This time though, there wasn't any laughter as my fellow students pitied my plight and probably thanked their lucky stars that their first name wasn't Albert.

Coach Forter must have decided that he wasn't yet done humiliating me. The third week came with a continuation of balancing chemical formulas. Only this time I unexpectedly followed an unplanned course of action. "Albert! Albert Stramiello! Go to the board, boy! Balance this equation for the class." I sat silently at my desk and stared straight ahead as he called my name again. Without any prior planning on my part, I slowly reached under my desk and picked up my books. I stood up from my desk and walked toward the board at the front of the room. But, then, I made a slow and deliberate left turn toward the classroom door. With my hand on the doorknob I could hear Coach Forter's deep, gruff voice, "Albert! Albert Stramiello! Where are you going, boy? I said go to the board." Without looking back, I closed the door behind me and proceeded to the guidance counselor's office.

Although Coach Forter may not have taught me how to balance a chemical formula, I did learn a very important lesson about treating students with respect and dignity. I am firmly convinced that teachers, whether they are at the elementary school level or in a university classroom, should not use their position of power and authority to ridicule students. The essence of excellence in teaching is having the ability to develop a learner-supportive classroom in which all students are treated with respect and dignity. A classroom should be a place of comfort and support for all learners. It should be a place where students should feel comfortable in acknowledging that they can't do something or that they are having difficulty mastering a concept. The instructor's role is to facilitate the student's acquisition of knowledge by serving as the living link between the learner and knowledge.

My joyful passion for teaching is both intense and immensely fulfilling. I am certain that I have followed the best career path for me. When I open my paycheck at the end of the month, I laugh as I think to myself, "I can't believe that they actually pay me to teach." As a matter of fact, I laugh heartily. I am a teacher!

Science Is Hard

Catherine M. Gardner, Ph.D.

I started life in a small, close-knit community. In my world, music reigned. My mom played the flute in high school, and my uncle was a renowned band director. While still a young child, I began piano lessons and, by the age of eight, started playing the flute. I was considered a child with great promise to become an exceptional musician. In the seventh grade, I auditioned for the high school band and became the youngest person to be a member of the award winning Parker High School Band. All-State Band, the Greenville Little Symphony, and other music honors followed. It was generally accepted that I was on the way to "making it big" in the world of music, even at the professional level. Then, I met Ms. Birdie Miller, a biology teacher at Parker High School.

Parker High School was a huge school with a special program for gifted and talented students. Participating students were given the freedom to go to any classes they felt they needed. If I was having difficulty in geometry, I could sit in geometry classes all day. Or, if I was working on a project in English, I could stay in the library all day. It was a short-lived program, as most high school students were not sufficiently mature to make good independent decisions on their participation in the program. However, I took full advantage of the program and, as a result the experience changed the course of my life.

At this time, my beloved grandmother was diagnosed with cancer. I was enrolled in my tenth-grade biology class and was required to develop and complete a science fair project. I decided that I would cure cancer as my science fair project! Enter Ms. Birdie Miller, my teacher and my continuing inspiration. Of course, I should do a science fair project on cancer, and, yes, I could do the research that may cure cancer. I set about researching the causes of cancer. With lots of guidance, I decided to cure pea plants of *Agrobacterium tumefaciens*.

Ms. Miller ordered the bacterium for me. I developed a working knowledge of culturing the bacterium. I felt like a doctor—preparing nutrient agar, sterilizing test tubes and agar, and using the sterilized materials to grow the *Agrobacterium tumefaciens*. I soaked my pea plant seeds and planted them in potting soil. Being certain to have replications and controls, I inoculated the pea plants with the bacterium. To my amazement, the plants developed crown gall, the disease caused by the bacterium. It produces a tumor-like growth that eventually kills the host plants. I tried antibiotics, ultraviolet light, heat, and alcohol to cure the plant cancer. Of course, all my plants died of crown gall disease, and I did not cure cancer. But, the entire experience with the excitement, intrigue, discovery, and intellectual pursuit of knowledge changed my life.

During my eleventh-grade year, I pulled together my parents, band director, and private music teachers and announced that I was going to stop my music and become a scientist. The reaction of these important people in my life was one of shock and disbelief. They saw talent, years of work, and potential being wasted. Many hours were spent trying to convince me of my mistake. With the certainty that only teenagers possess, I put down my flute and closed the cover on the piano. I was now on a quest to learn and do science. After all, I had not yet cured cancer!

I began working at the Food Science Department at Clemson University and decided to go to East Carolina University to major in biology. I worked as a lab assistant in the microbiology lab while in college. When I graduated, I was intent on working in a research lab to continue my passion for finding solutions to some of the problems of mankind. My husband was in graduate school, and I was to be the primary source of income. In 1971 I could work in a science laboratory for $5,000 a year, or I could teach science for $8,000. Yes, you have just met one of the few people who went into teaching for the money! My first teaching job was in a small, rural, impoverished school in eastern North Carolina.

Much to my surprise, I loved teaching science. I taught sixth- through twelfth-grade science. I would start my day with students watching *Spirogyra* (algae) under a microscope. One student found a strange-looking *Spirogyra*. It turns out those algae were having sex. I thought the building would flip as all the students rushed to watch sexual reproduction of algae. In chemistry we would check the chemical reactivity of halides by blowing up a piece of sodium as we placed it in water. I allowed each class to autograph the damage dome to the ceiling by their sodium. I truly believed that if I spent a day without my students actively involved in science, I was a failure. I still possess that belief.

I had found my home. I loved sharing my passion for science with these students. They loved science, and that, in turn, fueled my joy of teaching. Even though the call of research was still there, I was happy and content to spend the rest of my life teaching science in eastern North Carolina. Life sometimes changes plans. My husband was offered an assistantship at Clemson University to work on his Ph.D. We decided to move to Clemson, South Carolina. Now, I had the opportunity to return to research. But I was also offered a teaching position at a local junior high school. I did a summer of research and very quickly got tired counting bacteria on slides. I longed for the creativity, diversity of experiences, and interactions with my students. I missed teaching science.

At this point, I took the position of science teacher at the local junior high and renewed my joy and love of teaching. I had accelerated classes and a class of thirty-five ninth-graders who could not read and could only write their names. The accelerated classes were fun, but my joy of teaching came from the students who had so many challenges in life. I revamped the class to where it was totally hands-on learning with oral exams. It was physically exhausting, but these students for the first time in their lives experienced success. They knew their science and loved it. I had no discipline problems with this class. They loved the class and, as a result, loved me. I became very involved in all aspects of their lives and remain in touch with a few of them. Of all the blessings of my life, these students are one of the greatest joys I have experienced (so far).

Again, I had found my home, and it was teaching science. My husband took a position with the University of Georgia, and our son was born. I retired from teaching to be a stay-at-home mom. That lasted for about a year and then I returned to teaching on the college level. Now, I have the opportunity to share my passion for teaching with teachers who will pass it on to their students.

I want my students to feel the excitement and joy of science that I do. Most of the students with whom I interact enter my classes with the attitude that science is hard. They have years of believing that they cannot "do science." To overcome these obstacles is now my goal.

I believe that one must first possess the passion for teaching to share that gift with their students. My classroom is immersed in the joy of doing science. Primarily, I use discrepant events and gross facts to ignite that wonder about the world that I wish for my students.

Discrepant events are a natural in science. I have walked into the classroom with a Mickey Mouse umbrella chastising the students for not dressing appropriately. It will soon rain in this classroom, and I am the only one with an umbrella. That sparks the discussion of how it can rain inside the classroom. Another favorite discrepant event is when I use Vicki Cobb's book *Bet You Can't*. We go into the hallway and line up with heels against the wall. I use the bet you can't touch your toes challenge. No one can touch their toes, and they want to know why. We go into a discussion of center of mass and rotational inertia. Then, we go back into the classroom where I introduce the same concepts in the traditional manner, using overheads and mathematical concepts. My favorite discrepant event is the first night of class. Instead of starting class with the traditional introductions and reviewing the syllabus, I start class with a "Murder in the Lab" activity. The students are asked to solve the crime. At the end of the class, I ask them what they have learned. Students realize that they have learned the scientific method, cells, and the true nature of science without a textbook or white board. Then, we contrast the traditional teaching methods they have experienced in learning the scientific method. Most agree that the use of discrepant events awakens the curiosity so that students want to learn the science that explains their questions.

Most older elementary- and middle-grade students love to learn gross facts. Science has so many sources of information to grab students' attention and interest. I use pictures and storytelling to demonstrate how these resources can be used to "turn students on to" learning science. I have accumulated pictures of various intestinal parasites in humans. I accent those pictures with stories from sources such as *New Guinea Tapeworms and Jewish Grandmothers: Tales of Parasites and People* by Robert S. Desowitz. In this book, Desowitz describes how a 40-foot tapeworm may cause little discomfort except perhaps you could refer to yourself in the imperial style of "we." My students say, "Gross," and then they laugh. Then they want to know if this really happened. At this point, they are eagerly and actively learning about parasites. Another gross laboratory is to review the filth and contamination in the students' food. We use FDA sources to see the possibilities. This leads to continued self-directed learning where students will learn about pollution, processing, and animal farming.

My passion for teaching starts with my love of science. All the teaching techniques in the world cannot substitute for a teacher who lacks passion for the subject. When a teacher exudes the joy and wonder of the subject, students pick up it.

To bring students into the joy of teaching is our quest. The cycle of sharing your passion and then seeing that passion in your students is wonderful. Their joy and passion is the catalyst that continues our lifelong learning. I hope that I will be able to pass on the gift that Ms. Birdie Miller gave to me.

Miss Abney

Carolyn Garvin, Professor

What kindles the desire to teach? Is it love of a subject and the great joy that comes from sharing that love? Is it love of learning—the lifelong process of acquiring knowledge and, perhaps, wisdom? Is it love of "schooling"—working with the young to lead them to discover, perceive, experience, and know? Is it love of the young—the desire to pass on to them the traditions and the wisdom of the ages and to discover with them the wonder of the future? I contend that the desire to teach is kindled by a person who combines all of these loves and who, one day, enters the life of a young person and invites him or her into that transforming experience we call education.

I sat in the middle of the bed in my college dorm reading the news clippings sent to me by my mom. The fire that had destroyed my old elementary school had made the headlines, and in reading about the hometown tragedy, I was caught up in waves of nostalgia. In musing about my school and about those long ago days, I drifted back to old memories...

The sun was streaming through the long windows of the fourth-grade classroom on the second floor of Winship School. The sign on the door said, "Miss Martha Abney." I ventured into the room feeling very alone, for my family had moved into the area near the end of the previous school year, and I knew very few people. To make matters worse, I had begun to wear glasses recently, a condition that made me feel even more awkward and that made me feel that I stood out from everyone else. The tall figure who stood by the windows was almost a silhouette because of the brightness of the sun, but the sun glinted off bright red hair. When she turned to greet me, I saw a face accentuated by freckles and a wide smile. She asked my name, pinned on a name tag, led me to a desk, and turned to greet others who were entering the room. Some, like me, were alone; others were with parents or brothers and sisters. I sat quietly, not turning or looking around, not greeting friends, just waiting. Finally, the flurry of the opening morning ended, and we settled down to listen to Miss Abney. She explained the rules and procedures, handed out papers to complete, and engaged the class in a variety of opening activities within a matter of minutes. Though I was busily engaged in these directed activities, I was just as busily engaged in avoiding eye contact with everyone, especially with Miss Abney.

While my kindergarten, first-grade, and second-grade experiences had been days of wonder and fulfillment, in third grade, the new kid had learned that if you sat quietly and didn't call attention to yourself, you could make it through the school day without creating problems for a teacher who didn't like disruptions, such as a new student, to her established routine or to her schedule. So, I sat in my assigned desk on this first day of the new school year, with eyes downcast, working on the assignment that had been given to us. From the perspective of looking down, I saw a pair of shoes next to my desk—too large for a classmate—and

I looked up. Miss Abney was standing next to my desk. She leaned over, her red hair falling forward, and took my paper. I waited, horrified, wondering what I had done wrong. Then, she put the paper back on my desk, leaned forward once again, whispered, "Beautiful," and beamed at me. Her eyes connected with mine, and I found myself smiling back. She patted my hand and walked to the next desk, leaving me enveloped in the warmth of her smile.

Miss Abney, I later discovered, had been teaching fourth grade for some years, yet I had the feeling that she was timeless. I hurried to school each day anxious to discover what the day would bring. The usual—reading, arithmetic, language, geography, history, science—didn't seem so ordinary coming from Miss Abney. She drew me into discovery of numbers, words, places, people, and events. She led me into worlds I did not know: worlds of creativity and imagination and expression, worlds of fact and fiction. Her enthusiasm was contagious. I caught that enthusiasm and pushed myself to make Miss Abney proud. She could beam a smile straight into my fourth-grade heart and catch me up in learning without my realizing how much I was really learning.

My favorite time of day came after lunch when Miss Abney read to us. We all listened, heads on desks, as she brought characters to life. We cried with Lassie (*Lassie, Come Home*) and struggled to pull that sled with Buck (*Call of the Wild*); our imaginations were stirred by Johnny Tremaine and Hiawatha; we laughed at the adventures of Tom Sawyer and Eloise. In reading to us as a class, Miss Abney ignited a spark in me that grew into a flaming desire to read more, thus opening the door to the magic found in literature and in books of all kinds. That love for reading is still burning within me, and I seldom go on a trip, go to bed, or pass a day without reading something for the sheer pleasure of entering the magical world of literature in some form.

That year in the fourth grade passed so quickly; it seemed that we had started one week and ended the next. But instead of September, it was June, and it was time to move to the fifth grade. Miss Abney stood before us; once again the sunlight glinted off that red hair. We all sat very straight and still as she told us how proud she was of all that we had accomplished. I really don't remember all she said that day, but I remember thinking I want to be like Miss Abney; I wanted to be a teacher just like her. I had no idea of the import of those words; it was only later that I could identify my childish wish as a real desire to teach, to share my love of history, and to open the doors of discovery.

I spent the next twelve years completing my formal education. I achieved my goal of becoming a teacher. There were times in my college years when I briefly entertained the idea of another profession, but Miss Abney always drifted back into my thoughts. I tried to learn my craft: I attended seminars and conferences; I observed master teachers; I talked with education professionals. I learned that to be like Miss Abney, to reach my students in the way that she reached me, was a complex mix of my subjects, my students, and me. I could not give name to that complex mix until I encountered the work of Parker Palmer. In *The Courage to Teach*, Palmer states, "Good teachers possess a capacity for connectedness." He says that good teachers "are able to weave a complex web of connections among themselves, their subjects, and their students so that students can learn to weave a world for themselves."[1] All the pieces fell into place. Day by day, Miss Abney had been weaving a web of connections that drew me in and, at the same time, opened pathways that led me to the freedom to question, explore, dialogue, learn. The qualities she possessed went beyond skills and knowledge, beyond her degrees and her certification; she led me to learn to weave a world for myself, and so she made a difference in my life and set me on a path that called me to teach.

I often hear the students in my class, Introduction to Teaching, refer to the desire to make a difference in the lives of the students they plan to teach. There are few statements that imply more than the statement that one wishes to make a difference in another's life. Yet there are few statements that are as vague or as nebulous as that one. How does one make a difference? How does one enter the life of a student and draw him or her into the world of learning? How does one establish the connectedness that Palmer describes, that connectedness that I felt with Miss Abney, the tie that leads to making a difference. How did she weave that web of connections among herself, her subjects, and me so that I could learn to weave a world for myself?

In pondering those questions, I thought about Miss Abney and about other great teachers I have been privileged to have. I thought about my years of teaching sixth-graders, ninth-graders, juniors and seniors in high school. Thinking back over those years does not answer the questions nor does that reflection answer how or whether I made a difference in the life of a student. Memories evoked from class pictures or

---

[1] Parker J. Palmer, *The Courage to Teach: Exploring the Inner Landscape of a Teacher's Life* (San Francisco: Jossey-Bass, 1998) 11.

old yearbooks do not provide answers. Yet there is evidence that there was an impact, that connectedness was established. Evidence comes in various forms: letters, phone calls, cards, reunions, chance meetings, planned meetings, and E-mail messages out of the blue. But even these encounters do not provide the hard evidence of the concept named connectedness or why there is connectedness with one student and not another.

In searching for a more tangible description, I remembered an almost forgotten quote, "What is essential is invisible to the eye." I pulled out my copy of *The Little Prince* by Antoine de Saint-Exupéry and re-read the story, whose meaning for me evolved from a child's story to a meaningful parable of life. In the story, the Little Prince encounters many persons, places, and things in his travels. One of his encounters involves a small fox with whom he spends some days. In the story, the fox tells the Little Prince, "It is only with the heart that one can see rightly; what is essential is invisible to the eye.... It is the time you have wasted for your rose that makes your rose so important."[2] For me, an epiphany as to the meaning of connectedness emerged, an epiphany as to my relationship with Miss Abney, an epiphany as to the relationships with my own students. To me, "the time you have wasted" meant the time spent with Miss Abney and the time spent with my own students: the time together—laughing, listening, learning, discovering, talking, sharing, learning how the lift of an eyebrow or the wave of a hand or the hint of a smile can send an unspoken message. It

---

[2] Antoine de Saint-Exupéry, *The Little Prince* (New York: Harcourt, Brace, and World, 1943) 70.

is the enthusiasm, the joy, the deep emotion transmitted from one to another because of the love one has for subject, for learning, for schooling, for the young. These essentials that are invisible to the eye are the things that weave the fabric that connects us with our students. And as the fox said to the Little Prince, "It is only with the heart that one can see rightly," so it is that those connections we make are held in our hearts—what Palmer identifies as the place where our intellect, our emotions, our spirit, and our will converge[3]—and we have a chance to become teachers who make a difference.

So what kindles the desire to teach? For me, it was a person—Miss Martha Abney—who entered my life and who invited me into the learning experience we call education. It was the time I spent with her in that fourth-grade classroom where she shared love for her subjects and her joy in sharing that love; where she shared her love of learning with eight- and nine-year-olds; where she worked with us to lead us to discover, to perceive, to experience, and to know; where she "wasted" time with us to lead us to an appreciation of the traditions and wisdom of the ages and to instill in us a sense of wonder for the future; where she kindled in me the desire to become a teacher who makes a difference.

---

[3] Palmer, *The Courage to Teach*, 11.

Making a Difference

H. Anne Hathaway, Ed.D.

I have a true passion for teaching. To me, teaching is the most noble of callings, the greatest of professions, superseding medicine and law. When I reflect on the respect and value given to doctors and lawyers by society, I am reminded of the probable reason—each addresses the immediate need of an individual and usually results in a fairly immediate outcome or resolution. For a doctor's efforts, a patient either gets well or does not; either the patient lives or dies. The lawyer wins, loses, or settles a case. The result is known to the doctor or lawyer and to the patient or client. Such is not the situation for a teacher. Learning is a lifelong process. Therefore, having moved through my career as a classroom teacher, system-level subject area coordinator, state-level subject area consultant, higher education teacher, and higher education administrator, I find myself, at this point in time, having returned to my passion—teaching.

I am an idealist who believes every teacher should be one also. This idealism is believing that I can and do make a difference in the life of an individual and in society, both directly and indirectly. The personal interaction I have with individual students provides me the opportunity to help students develop the knowledge bases and skills that will enable them to continue learning when necessary and for the simple enjoyment of learning. Simultaneously, I have the opportunity to enable students to become contributing members of society, which, in turn, perpetuates a thinking society that is sensitive to the needs of its members and to its own entity. Moreover, as a teacher-education professor, I idealistically believe that I contribute to this directly and indirectly. Because I teach, I have direct interaction with students and, thus, have a direct influence on their lives. However, because my students are prospective and practicing teachers, I affect the lives of their students. The exponential effect of my teaching is a scenario that causes me to pause and realize that I will never know the actual impact I have today and will have in the future. Therefore, the "difference I make" must be positive, appropriate, and flexible enough to accommodate an ever-changing society. These thoughts neither inhibit me nor diminish my idealism. Rather, "the difference I make" becomes a serious responsibility that perpetuates my idealism. Once I lose that idealism, it is time for me to step away from teaching.

This idealism leads me to my passion to enable American *democracy* to survive and thrive. For this to be, there must be a knowledgeable and critical thinking citizenry. Having skills and knowledge to "function effectively" in society is a worthy goal; yet, it is a minimal goal that, while possibly maintaining democracy, does not necessarily enable it to thrive. For America's form of government to move forward, the citizenry must be comprised of people who are critical thinkers, who want to know both sides of an issue, and who can make decisions for themselves. The citizens of this country must be unwilling to accept "plausible fiction" and "false truths" without analysis and synthesis and must be unwilling to accept "truths" and "facts" given by politicians, celebrities, ministers, and the wealthy, for example, simply because of their positions or status. Americans must be active participants in the political process, in the welfare of the union and its citizens, and in the maintenance of integrity and justice. They must find creative ways to resolve conflict within this country and between this country and another. They must examine in a critical and rational manner the economics, laws, and opportunities in this country to reverse the increasing number of people in poverty and the widening gap between the wealthy and the poor. They must believe they can make a difference and, thus, must move away from apathy. To do all this, they must be critical thinkers with good problem-solving abilities.

Education plays a critical role in the flourishing of a democracy, especially since teaching can directly and indirectly enable the actualization of a citizenry that believes in, promotes, and actively participates in the democratic form of government. Thus, I come now to my passion for being a catalyst for thinking, molding the mind of the individual. The human being has a cognitive ability not yet found to exist in other animals. It is that ability and brain with which the teacher works. As a teacher, I am awed with having the power to enable changes in brain synapses and in cognition. Moreover, I may never truly know what changes I have effected and if these changes were positive or negative. Yes, a test tells me some of the changes; but I have no knowledge of the long-term effects I might have had on an individual, on the students they teach, and ultimately on society. This concept enhances my passion for teaching. If I make a difference and do not know explicitly what that difference is or will be, then I am committed to assisting students in their move toward formal abstract thinking. I passionately want individuals to have questioning minds, not to accept ideas and concepts at face value, but to see the parts, the whole picture, and their relationships; to see both sides of an issue; to see patterns and relationships; to know something and be able to do something with understanding; and to make connections between and among ideas, concepts, facts, processes, and skills. I want individuals to be critical thinkers because, then, they will have actualized the capability that separates and distinguishes them on this earth. Thus, molding the mind through serving as a catalyst for thinking is not only an awesome responsibility but also a most noble vocation.

This idea of being a catalyst for thinking provides me the opportunities for facilitating understanding of a difficult concept or connection and for facilitating a new or different perspective. Being a catalyst also provides me a means for my true passion—finding the one or several questions that will spark the synapses and generate new connections.

The Socratic method of teaching through questioning rather than through telling has been a major influence on me and, as such, has affected my teaching and my interaction with students. From a very young age, I constantly have asked the question, "Why?"—always seeking to learn more about many different things and ideas. My curiosity has not abated; but, rather, it has been enhanced by the more I learn. Later, in a graduate course taught by a professor who had studied under Carl Rogers, this characteristic of questioning was joined with the Rogerian ideas of teaching. What a collision of ideas and pedagogy! On the one hand, I am a mathematics educator who understands and appreciates the inherent structure of the mathematics and believes, in many ways, that the discipline should be taught in a straight-forward, didactic manner. On the other hand, I am one who must understand the mathematics to know it, one who believes everyone must understand mathematics to learn it, and one who believes questioning is one of most effective means for understanding and learning.

Having the great desire to see students make connections and to facilitate their cognitive leaps in understanding, I believe questioning to be the most important of all pedagogical strategies. It is the vehicle that enables the various instructional models to be effective. Therefore, consistently through the years, I have made a conscious effort to improve my questioning skills because they, in turn, make me a more effective teacher.

The following are some questioning scenarios that have played out in some of my classes through the years:

Early Childhood Math Methods—The Circle
Why is this shape not a rectangle?
Name one characteristic of a rectangle.
Does this shape have that characteristic?
Why?
What is one characteristic of this shape?
What is another characteristic of this shape?
Are these characteristics similar to or unlike the characteristics of a rectangle?

This scenario is more cognitively effective than when the question, "What is the name of this shape?," is asked.

Middle-Grades   Math   Methods—Multiplication
Tables/Algebraic concepts

Table A	Table B
1 2 3	*1 2 3*
0x2=0	2x0=0
1x2=2	2x1=2
2x2=4	2x2=4
3x2=6	2x3=6
4x2=8	2x4=8

In Table A, column 1, what is the pattern?

In column 2, what is the pattern?

How is the pattern in column 3 like the pattern in column 1?

How is the pattern in column 2 like the patterns in columns 1 and 3?

Why?

In which columns do the numbers vary?

In which columns do the numbers remain constant?

Do the values in one of the columns depend on the values in another column?

In which column are the values dependent on numbers in another column?

In which column are the values independent from numbers in another column?

What are the similarities and differences between Tables A and B?

How can we generalize the relationships we have discussed?

These questions lead to an understanding of variable, constant, independent variable, and dependent variable without necessarily learning the vocabulary and instead of giving mathematical terms and definitions for memorization and recall with understanding to come later.

Middle-Grades Curriculum

Explain the relationship between middle-grades curriculum design and adolescent development.

Discuss the relationship between an advisor/advisee program and the four major academic areas.

Delineate and explain two possible contributions an advisor/advisee program makes to the four academic areas: language arts, mathematics, science, and social studies.

Including examples, explain whether a teacher can integrate the behaviorist and constructivist learning theories in the same middle school class/lesson.

Middle-Grades Math Methods

Discuss the relationship among concept development, drill and practice, and problem solving/application.

Explain why a square is each of the following: rhombus, rectangle, parallelogram, trapezoid, and quadrilateral.

Enabling me to facilitate higher levels of thinking in my students, these two sets of questions require the student to demonstrate understanding and find patterns and relationships through analysis and synthesis.

These are very simple examples of questioning that require a student to pull information from memory to use in a new learning experience; to move to a level of thinking above the recall level; to distinguish similarities and differences; to move toward more abstract, formal thought processes; to become more effective problem solvers; to draw conclusions with valid arguments; and to make sense of new knowledge through questioning rather than by being told.

This facilitation, through questioning, of student's understanding of new concepts and ideas and students' new perspectives and understandings of prior knowledge is a very exciting aspect of teaching for me. The more there are answers to my questions, the more questions I can and will generate, resulting in enriched learning and higher levels of critical thinking.

As I reflect on this discussion, I am aware that the essence of my passion for teaching is that I am a lifelong learner, yearning to know everything about an eclectic array of topics. I want to know more about how one learns, how one learns best, and mathematics; but I also want to know more about physics, space, the origins of man, genetics, archeology, sociology, religion, philosophy, history, current events, art, minerals and gemstones, music, and the relationships between and among these and other areas. Being a lifelong learner provokes me to want others to know what humans have learned and to experience the freedom that knowledge provides—the freedom to think without control by another, to have opinions, to make decisions, to solve problems, and to find and create new knowledge. This freedom ultimately is what separates man from all other beings, and it is this freedom that gives an individual power to control one's own destiny and to contribute to the progress of mankind. It is this freedom that a teacher, not a doctor or a lawyer, can facilitate.

When all is said and done and when my students are many years away from me, I hope they will remember me for my passion for teaching, my passion for my subject matter, my passion for questioning, my passion for provoking them to think in different and new ways and at levels more abstract than before, and my overriding belief that I make a difference in the lives of my students and in society.

Feels Like Coming Home

Margaret Rainey Morris, Ed.D.

I have always felt at home in the classroom. If home can be defined as that place where one finds, on one hand, acceptance and support and, on the other hand, challenge and disappointment, the classroom has provided this and more. Considering that teaching was what I always wanted to do when I grew up, understanding that this was initially not so much for the love of children or the love of a particular subject, indeed; the classroom provided the stability missing from my early years. Now, over a three-decade journey, at various levels of engagement and levels of teaching, that place, that home, has been and is the classroom, a place of on-going change, yet a place of continuity and the familiar.

Trying to understand and explain what has made the classroom that place of substance and passion for me is complex and firmly grounded in relationships—the relationship between teacher and the needs of the student; the heuristic, that is, the trial and error of the relationship with the environment of the classroom; and, of course, the evolving, ever-changing relationship between the pedagogy of the classroom and the teacher. When considering these three concepts that have played key roles in my remaining in teaching, my chosen vocation, they immediately bring to mind Frederick Buechner's observation of his life's vocation as "the place where your deep gladness meets the world's deep need."[1]

For me this place was first realized in the elementary classroom, in fact, in the first classroom that was truly mine—the classroom that demanded full responsibility and full accountability for and to the needs of the students assigned to me for that first year.

Understanding Each Other: The Teacher and the Student

That first year of full-time teaching was in a rural community. Forty-five students enrolled in my fifth-grade class that year. The room itself was typical; blackboard at the front of the room, bare bulletin boards on the inside wall, windows that opened horizontally across the outside wall, and two built-in cabinets for storage in the back that were joined by a metal pole with wire hangers for coats. The desks were arranged in six rows—wall-to-wall. Consequently, the walls of the traditional classroom strained with the presence of students as well as the old, clunky one-piece desks that offered little flexibility as far as grouping options. My plans for learning centers and a reading nook were initially jettisoned and eventually revised. This classroom, being the first classroom, with all of its limitations, held for me significance as the beginning of my life as a teacher, as well as the beginning of a phenomenon that occurred time and again—the phenomenon of negotiating place. The students of this class, who had been together most of their school

---

[1] Frederick Buechner, *Wishful Thinking: A Seeker's ABC* (San Francisco: Harper, 1993) 119.

career, played a role in moving me toward the understanding of what was necessary in this negotiation—the understanding that learning and teaching are reciprocal. Addie and Edward were part of this first class. Addie looked like her name. That is, her name reflected a time and a texture outside of the present era of the 1960s. In the age of the miniskirt, she wore a long, homemade dress, which touched her scuffed black and white oxfords; her long, but unfashionably tangled hair reminded one not of neglect, but of the lack of importance trends hold for those living in poverty. Although Addie struggled in every area of the fifth-grade course work that year, there remained a quiet but constant sweetness in her attitude toward school, toward her peers, and toward me. She was the first student for whom I knew I had made a difference.

Making meaning or finding understanding of those concepts needed by fifth-graders eluded Addie. Math, in particular, brought struggle and error to her day and frustration to mine. She seemed unresponsive to various strategies as well as to me as her teacher. Pleasant, but never smiling, she went through the day in silence. Could it be that telling and demonstrating to a student how a mathematical process worked was not enough? The other students understood her difficulty and always offered the help and encouragement that come with being in the same learning community. I slowly came to understand that I was the outsider, the one who had to find a way to meet the needs of this group—those needs that were better understood by the group itself than by the teacher.

One day, after a difficult lesson on working with fractions, the students were asked to go to the board to practice this new mathematical skill. When it was Addie's turn to work her problem along with others, I held my breath. As she slowly worked the assigned problem, the students encouraged her. They were not condescending, but supportive. When she had completed the problem, she turned to me. I immediately knew that the problem was correct. The smile on her usually unanimated face was the proof. She understood. At that moment, I felt as if I had found my place with these students. I had made a difference. As I confirmed the correctness of the math problem, a cheer went up from those around her. An experience that might have turned into a competitive disappointment for both Addie and I taught me the importance of teacher and student connection in the complex process of learning and teaching and the patience to wait for that connection to happen.

Sadly, Edward brought to that first year an example of disconnection between teacher and student, the stark reality that loss and missed opportunities can occur in the blinking of an eye. Edward was a quiet, smiling student, who spoke when spoken to; the kind of student who completed his work on time, found something else to do to occupy his time, and caused no trouble by talking or misbehaving. In other words, for a first-year teacher, he was easily lost among the forty-four other students in the class. One November morning, the principal came to my door and told me that Edward had died in his sleep the night before of a cerebral hemorrhage. As I told the class of Edward's death, the oddest thing happened. These ten-year-old students who had known Edward all of his short life began to console me. The shared identity they had with Edward enabled them to comfort an adult who barely knew or understood him.

Later that evening, my husband and I drove out of town into the country to visit with the family. After being greeted by Edward's mother and voicing condolences, she led us into Edward's bedroom. As customary, he was laid in his bed, covered, as if sleeping. Standing there, looking at this little boy, a child with whom I had barely connected, a deep feeling of regret enveloped me. A conviction emerged that building community and negotiating place, that is, understanding your place and identifying with your students within a classroom as well as the broader community, were central to the vocation of a teacher.

Finding Community: The Environment of the Classroom

The idea of building a community of learners is not a new one. From the time of the sophists, the notion of learners being led out by a teacher and coming together for the common purpose of learning has existed. However, as a first-year teacher, I was seeing the classroom from a very different perspective. I discovered that central to the concept of community was the important relationship between the teacher and the environment of the classroom and that special place this holds for the elementary teacher, indeed, a different meaning than for those teaching at the middle or the high school level. For these elementary students, the classroom became the home away from home. For many, the classroom became the only haven of safety experienced during the day, and for others, the classroom was definitely the only example of community they knew. That year, my forty-five fifth-graders remained in the same classroom all day with their desks becoming havens—sometimes visited, but never occupied by other students during the day.

Equally important to the concept of place was the feast provided for the senses within the classroom. Just as we equate home with the smell of coffee perking on the stove or freshly baked cookies, the classroom brought comfort through experiences that encompassed looking, smelling, touching, and moving.

The look of the classroom was important as to climate, but brought dilemma: to decorate or not to decorate, to stimulate or to promote quiet. Smells occupy the classroom like an invading army. Nothing smells like school supplies, especially new ones. The books, the pencil lead, the markers, all bring to mind the picture of projects, some finished and some unfinished. The slightly sour smell of perspiration from students returning from recess during the warmer days. The feel of the chalkiness of the blackboard, the gooeyness of paste, and of holiday ornament dough all added to the sensuous picture of the classroom.

Moving a class of forty-five from one place to another became an art and science. Creative organization resulted in the students actually being able to move about in order to work on independent projects. I quickly learned that the kinesthetic aspect of orchestrating or managing the classroom led to the joyful sound of work and cooperative motion when all was well and the inevitable joyless chaos and confusion when all was not well.

These familiar images brought to the students and to me an emotional safety net, for I still struggled somewhat in my effort to adjust to this classroom community and to the loss that had affected all of us. As the holiday season approached in December, we began to prepare the classroom by making ornaments for the tree. After giving directions and demonstrating the process of making the ornaments, we all settled into the quiet work of completing the project. From the back of the room, I soon heard the quiet singing of the old spiritual, "Soon and very soon, we are going to see the King," coming from a lone singer. As we continued to work, the singing continued with the students joining in one by one until all were quietly singing the spiritual as we worked. I smiled; we were together.

Finding Ethos: The Spirit of Pedagogy

"Having more than three reading groups is for the birds," echoed the words of my student-teaching cooperating teacher. During that first year of wall-to-wall students, these words rang true. In fact, finding a place to carry forth this particular way of teaching reading proved problematic. Like most beginning teachers, I was trying to teach as I had been taught, "All right, now it is time for social studies. Put your math book away and get out your social studies book." However, I was soon to learn that compartmentalizing instruction was contrary to how we as teachers eventually ask students to apply their learning. Through paying attention to the students and observing the learning processes that were occurring in the classroom, I found curricular connections and began the philosophical transition toward embracing the tenets of integrating the curriculum when appropriate.

Interestingly, this approach to curriculum led to a change in my belief system as to curriculum delivery. The spirit of the classroom had reflected the climate of teacher as sage, telling all, filling up the empty vessels. Through this change, I, as their teacher, became a partner in learning—a guide on the side. This change of attitude led to a camaraderie, a cooperative ethos, that I have attempted to replicate in the classrooms that followed. Not only were we partners in learning, but I gained appreciation and respect for the spirit of the students and the knowledge they brought to that classroom. When all was said and done, the classroom was and remains for me a place where all teach and learn.

Negotiating Place: Arriving and Knowing

Since that first year I have known many classrooms and many students. Addie and Edward remain with me from that first year as well as the life lessons learned. In one sense, although the setting is different and the students are older, I find myself arriving where I began. As T. S. Elliot's poem, *Little Giddings*, concludes, "We shall not cease from exploration / And the end of all our exploring / Will be to arrive where we started / And know the place for the first time."[2] The university setting has provided opportunities to negotiate my place from a not so different perspective. The classroom continues to offer the same sensibilities of that first one. A note recently received from a former student concluded, "Thank you for the 'sweet taste' you left in my mouth towards teacher education." Perhaps one can go home again.

---

[2] T. S. Elliot, "Little Gidding," *Collected Poems and Plays 1909–1950* (New York: Harcourt Brace, 1952) 27–30.

Making a Difference

Bruce Sliger, Ed.D.

Twenty years ago, I graduated from college with a degree in business (economics). With that degree in hand, I decided law school was the key to my economic future. I worked for a year to save sufficient money to attend law school. However, my life took an unexpected turn during that year. With few other job opportunities available, I took a position as a social services caseworker in Tennessee. Faced with the responsibility of counseling families on everything from nutrition to family planning, I had to ask myself what a twenty-six-year-old knows about family planning. In analyzing my social worker role, I realized much of what I was doing would fall under the category of teaching.

Meanwhile, at home my wife of three years continued her role as an elementary school teacher. She is one those people who knew from childhood that she wanted to be a teacher. Each day she would come home from work so excited about the things her students were doing and learning. I don't think I ever met anyone who loved her job as much. Between my work with the state and my wife's enthusiasm for what she did, I began to question what I wanted to do with my life. I finally decided to go back to college, not to get a law degree, but to major in secondary education. From my first class, it was clear I had made the right choice.

While in college, I was fortunate to have some of the finest professors help me develop my teaching skills. For example, I learned that a teacher could consciously create a positive classroom setting, a place where students would feel safe, so they could focus on learning. This simple, yet powerful idea has stayed with me over my entire career. Over the length of my entire career from the early public school teaching days to university professor, the concept of creating a positive setting in my classroom has remained a major goal. I remember reading the work of Seymour Sarason in my graduate classes and thinking how important the concept really is. Additionally, I learned how much of an impact a good teacher has on the lives of students. Sometimes teachers wonder and even question whether they are making a difference. The following stories constantly remind me, and I hope you, of just how much teachers and school leaders impact their students.

Background

During my career, I have worked as a reading teacher, social studies department chairperson, assistant principal at a high school and junior high, elementary school principal, middle school principal, and finally as an associate professor of graduate education. I have worked with students from kindergarten through graduate school. The totality of these experiences has greatly influenced my personal philosophy and methodology of teaching. For instance, my experiences suggest that instructing adults is a different type of teaching for several reasons. One is that adults come to class with their own perceptions, experiences, and knowledge of the world. These factors must be taken into account when structuring the course and considering the method of teaching. In preparing the curriculum for my graduate courses, I am compelled to consider a strong blend of educational theory and practical applications.

One of the first things I do is to ensure that the environment is conducive to promoting a "setting" that is non-threatening and non-judgmental where the learners have permission for, and are expected to, share in the responsibility for their learning. This climate encourages intellectual freedom where students are accepted and respected as intellectually experienced adults whose opinions are given credence and where their abilities and life achievements are acknowledged as being worthy of consideration.

My teaching techniques include lecture, class discussion, small-group work, and group projects. In addition, I have incorporated technology into the courses I teach. For example, students are grouped (interdisciplinary teams) and assigned middle school topics to research. Each group presents their findings to the class using a PowerPoint presentation at the end of the course. These learning groups demonstrate the same type of experience teachers need to use with middle-grades students. This opportunity to work with prospective teachers to develop their knowledge and skills is extremely rewarding for me.

I can relate to many of our nontraditional students at the university because my career path was similar to theirs. Many hold jobs during the day and come to class at night because they want to become teachers. Some will take a pay cut (sometimes a major one) to enter a profession they believe will be more rewarding. I have the highest regard for these future teachers. The vast majority of them will become excellent teachers. Like me, they will tell you themselves after a few years this was the best decision they ever made.

Finally, I have always strongly believed in teacher leadership. Katzenmeyer and Moller define teacher leadership as: "Teachers who are leaders lead within and beyond the classroom, identify with and contribute to a community of teacher learners and leaders, and influence others toward improved educational practice."[1] The following stories reflect what can happen when teachers and school leaders come together to create a positive school setting and work together to address the needs of their students.

The Stories

I remember the day I completed my teacher preparation program and with teaching certificate clutched in hand, I set out to find a teaching position. A large Atlanta school district was interviewing on campus. The interview went very well and the district's director of personnel asked me to contact his office in two weeks. I was thrilled by the prospect of being hired in one of the finest school systems in the southeast. Two weeks later when I made the call to the personnel office, I was asked to come to Atlanta for a further interview. The initial interview in Atlanta went well and I was sent out to

---

[1] Marilyn Katzenmeyer and Gayle Moller, Awakening the Sleeping Giant: Helping Teachers Develop as Leaders, 2nd ed. (Thousand Oaks CA: Corwin Press, 2001).

interview with three different high school principals. Two of the high schools were regular high school situations. The third was an alternative high school for students expelled from one of the regular high schools. I was impressed with the principal of the alternative school. He appeared to me to be very concerned about his students and the entire alternative school program.

After the three interviews, I went back to the county personnel office as directed. To my surprise, the director of personnel said all three principals wanted to hire me for a teaching position in social studies. He asked me which school I liked the best. Before I could respond, he said the alternative school principal really wanted me at his school. The director went on to say that he thought I would like working with the principal and faculty. I told him I was excited by the prospect of working with the wonderful people I had met at the alternative school.

As an aside I should add that my wife was also able to share in my good fortune. As part of the final interview, I happened to mention to the director that my wife was an elementary school teacher. In fact, she was a big reason I decided to go into teaching. When I accepted my teaching position, the director asked to speak to my wife. In the end, she was hired to teach in an elementary school that same day.

It did not take long to realize how fortunate I really was. The principal and teachers at the alternative school were outstanding people and master teachers. They took me under their wing right from the beginning. As I reflect over my career, I realize this experience was one of the best I could have had. The principal and faculty were totally dedicated to turning around as many students as they could. The impact these people had on the lives of students was truly amazing. I learned so much about teaching while working with at-risk kids during my first few years at this school.

After completing the alternative school program (usually one or two quarters), many students requested to stay at the alternative school because it was the first time they had ever been successful in school. To see students go from all F's to good grades with a desire to learn is as good as it gets for a teacher. I initiated an honor role for students who brought their grades up. I posted the honor role on my door each week. Every Monday morning students would gather outside my door before class to see who made it. These were students who had never been successful in school with the right motivation.

I remember in particular one young man who came in with a real attitude, not unlike many of his peers. However, he began to change and soon became an excellent student. His grades greatly improved and so did his attitude. He told me that it was the first time he had ever done well in school, yet he was afraid if he went back to his old school he would simply get back into trouble because his old teachers would not believe he could be successful. Still, there was little I could do to help him. The alternative school program was not set up to permit a student to stay permanently at the school. I presented the problem to the faculty and they came up with an alternative solution. The young man would be allowed to attend a different high school. He liked this option. Later we did a follow-up to see how he was doing. We were told this young man was doing fine.

Now the Rest of the Story

A few years later at Christmastime, my wife and I were walking through Macy's, when I heard someone call my name. I turned around to find a tall young man walking quickly toward me. He asked: "Do you remember me?" Here was my special student who wanted to go to a different high school. He wanted to thank me and all of the other teachers who had helped him. He explained that he worked hard and graduated from high school. He went on to say he was accepted into college at a local university. I asked him about his major? He looked at me and said: "Mr. Sliger, I thought you knew. I am going to be a teacher. I hope one just like you."

Let me share another story with you that happened while I was an assistant elementary principal. I had been asked to be the principal at a new elementary school. The opportunity to open a new school was very appealing to me. I decided to accept the challenge on one condition (I wasn't in a very strong bargaining position but decided to try). I wanted the final say on hiring of all staff members. From early in my career, I realized how important strong teachers are to student learning, so it was a very important condition to me. To my surprise, I was given the right to do my own hiring.

Given the chance, I stole, I mean hired, the best teachers from many different schools. A majority of students slated to attend this school would come from "the projects." Before I started I was warned that traditionally the parents of these students had not been very involved in their children's education. We both agreed that something had to be done to change this attitude if we were going to make a difference in the lives of these children. I thought a good place to start would be to present the problem to the faculty. After much discussion we came up with several ideas for increasing parent involvement.

The Plan

Since many of our parents did not have transportation, on PTA nights we wanted our bus drivers to drive their routes and pick up parents and students. I contacted the director of transportation to explain the plan. His response was there was no money in the budget to pay the drivers and raised vague concerns about possible liability issues. Not to be thwarted, I called the superintendent and explained the situation. He said he would get back to me. A few minutes later the director of transportation called me to say he could make the necessary arrangements. Thank goodness for superintendents that will support initiatives for children.

The next morning I was in my office very early doing paperwork, when I was paid a surprise visit by not one, but all nine bus drivers serving the school. One bus driver can change your day as an administrator. But nine at one time? They filed into my office and began to explain that they had heard about our plan to run the buses into "the projects" to pick up parents and students on PTA nights. I was thinking here it comes now.

They explained that they had talked it over and that they would drive the buses at no cost to the county! They went on to say that they believed this was a good idea and wanted to contribute their share. The bus drivers, custodians, cafeteria ladies were all a part of our team. Everybody was given school t-shirts. By the way, when I left the school for a college teaching position, the bus drivers presented me a trophy with a school bus on top thanking me for all the support. I still have this trophy in my office to remind me of those wonderful people.

The next part of the plan was simple but important. If you feed them they will come. We provided food (a very nice spread) to all of our parents and students. Did I mention door prizes? Yes, we had donations from several local businesses. Each parent was given a ticket with a number on it. During the meeting we would pull out a ticket and read the number. The winner would happily step up to claim the prize. I remember at one PTA meeting a local travel agency had donated a free weekend at one of Atlanta's exclusive hotels (including breakfast). The tension mounted as we began our drawing. What happened next may have been divine intervention.

The school was fortunate to have many loyal and supportive parents. However, there was one family from day one, who attended every meeting, spaghetti dinner, and family night. The wife even volunteered at school. They were a hard-working couple, yet they barely made ends meet. They drove a beat-up old car, yet did all they could to support their children and the school. Yes, they won the drawing. I will never forget the look on their faces. What a great night!

Lastly, I told the PTA president that PTA meetings could last no longer than fifteen minutes. Have you ever gone to a PTA meeting and sat on those hard little chairs for hours? Treating parents like that, it is not surprising that they do not come back. After the meeting parents were invited to visit with their son's or daughter's teacher. This proved to be a worthwhile undertaking.

When the time was up, I made an announcement that the buses would leave in fifteen minutes. Each time I would ride a different bus to and from the meeting in order to chat with the parents. One of the most rewarding moments in my career came when a very large lady a few seats back called my name. "Dr. Sliger, I want you to know how much we appreciate you making us feel welcome at the school. I have never gone to a school before. I know that the only way my son is going to get out of the projects is by that there school. You have my support!"

She then turned to her very thin, small son sitting in the same seat and told him in no uncertain terms: "You're in big trouble boy. You've been telling me that you have no homework every night. Your teacher told me that was why you are failing." The little boy just looked straight ahead (probably a wise course of action). The mother went on: "Dr. Sliger, he is going to do his homework." And she kept her promise. The young man's grades went from D's and F's to B's very quickly.

The program worked so well that we had 300 to 500 parents attend our PTA meetings and the teachers saw major improvement in the attitude, not to mention the quality of work. At the end of the year, students who scored the lowest in the county on standardized tests were now close to the top. It all goes to show that when parents and teachers work together they can accomplish almost anything in education.

Today I am a college professor at a great university where we have a positive approach to training our teachers to realize their potential to make a significant difference in this wonderful career. In fact, Mercer's conceptual framework is all about the transforming practitioner. The framework states:

"The Transforming Practitioner," the living link between the child and learning, is the educator who is changing internally through understanding, practicing, and reflecting such that, individually and collaboratively, he or she implements for all children appropriate and significant life-changing learning experiences that effectively provide for the needs of the whole child, actively engage students in the learning process, and promote life-long learning.

It is my desire to assist and in some small way to prepare teachers who will truly reflect these practices in their everyday classrooms. It is imperative that student teachers learn that if they work in conjunction with their school leaders, they can create a positive learning environment that will make a significant difference in the lives of children. After all, teachers can be leaders too and most importantly teachers make a difference.

The Teacher I Continue to Become:

A Loving Tribute to Those Who Have Taught Me

William O. Lacefield, III, Ed.D.

I know that I was born to teach. Even as a very young child, I would line up my stuffed animals on the floor and read to them, ask questions of them (and imagine the answers that I might have received from human students), and demonstrate addition and subtraction exercises on a small chalk board I had excitedly received as a Christmas gift. I think I enjoyed "playing school" so much because I tremendously enjoyed being a student. Even from my first day of school, learning was a pleasure—and a definite passion—for me. I remember attending a preschool program at a church in Louisville, Kentucky. My teachers were Miss Jean and Miss Betty and I thought they were some of the most wonderful people in the world. I clearly remember many of the learning activities they planned for my fellow students and me. We drew and colored pictures, made all sorts of arts and crafts, and practiced identifying shapes and colors. We sang a variety of enjoyable songs. (My favorite was "I'm a Little Teapot." I found such fun in "acting out" the song by forming my body into the shape of a teapot and pretending to pour the tea.) I still have an imprint of my hand that I made in a pie plate of plaster of Paris during my preschool experience. Yes, Miss Jean and Miss Betty put forth great efforts to make learning engaging, fun, and memorable. When the academic year ended, I was a bit sad. I wanted to continue going to school and I'm sure I asked my parents many times when I could go to school again. The time to begin first grade soon arrived, and I was most excited. My mother drove me to the school and went to the classroom with me. I vividly remember that several of the other boys and girls were crying and complaining that they did not wish to be there. I did not understand why children would be sad about having to attend first grade, and I asked my mother, "Why are so many people crying?" She explained that they did not yet know how interesting and enjoyable school was going to be. I, though, was very hopeful and looked forward to many wonderful school days.

Today, as I reflect on my days as a student in grades one through twelve, I can honestly say that I remember every single teacher by name and appearance. I remember the ones I considered to be "nice" teachers and the few who, in my estimation, could have been nicer. Mrs. Bottoms, my first-grade teacher, was a huge believer in phonics. In her class we were given numerous coloring sheets and were asked to color pictures of items whose names, for example, began with the "tr" sound or ended with the "ng" sound. Mrs. Bottoms also believed in spanking—and I must admit that I was spanked by Mrs. Bottoms on more than one occasion. I don't remember all of the reasons for my spankings, but I do know that once, I stayed in the cafeteria after lunch to assist with the wiping of the tables. It is not that we were not allowed to stay and help wipe the tables; we were, in fact, required to do so, but only on days that we were assigned to do so. I explained to Mrs. Bottoms that I was only trying to help, but my attempted reasoning was to no avail. I still received at least two "licks." Mrs. Keller was my third-grade teacher. I remember her as a petite woman who became pregnant during the school year. I also remember my excitement when we began to learn cursive handwriting. I enjoyed practicing writing and could hardly wait until we had learned to write all of the letters in my name. (Mrs. Keller had established a rule that once the class had studied how to write all of the letters in a student's name, he or she could begin writing his or her name in cursive on all assignments.) I also enjoyed learning the multiplication tables. Mrs. Keller, a somewhat progressive teacher for the time, set up what she called "learning stations" throughout the classroom. Each station featured a different activity or game designed to make it easier for us to recall the multiplication facts. I cannot remember the details of all the games, but I know that my favorite made use of dice and playing cards as identifiers of the factors that we were to multiply. Mrs. Basham was my fifth-grade teacher. She loved literature and read to us every day. I had enjoyed reading before I met Mrs. Basham, but I must admit that she truly nurtured my enjoyment of fiction as well as non-fiction. I remember that in her classroom, she had a special set of *Readers' Digest* magazines that had been especially designed for young readers. On certain days, we were assigned to read stories or articles from these magazines. I felt so "grown up," reading the same magazine (or so I thought) that my beloved grandmother very much enjoyed.

During the summer between my sixth- and seventh-grade years, my family moved from Louisville, Kentucky, to Macon, Georgia. It took me a while to become accustomed to some of my teachers' Southern accents. During a spelling bee at the beginning of the school year, my homeroom teacher asked me to spell what I heard as "patrotism." I even asked her if she had said, "patrotism." "Yes, patrotism," she answered. So, I spelled what I had heard—"p-a-t-r-o-t-i-s-m." Of course, the teacher indicated that I had misspelled the word and went on to say that I had omitted an "i." I was most upset, as I knew exactly how to spell "patriotism." I just did not think that was the word that I was being asked to spell. (It did not take me long to learn to understand—and to speak with—a Southern accent.) Ms. Brown was my mathematics teacher in seventh grade. Although I had always performed well in mathematics, I never really came to a realization of how much I enjoyed mathematics until I met Ms. Brown. She was excited about all aspects of mathematics and did all she could to transfer the excitement to her students. I felt incredibly honored when Ms. Brown asked me to join the school's mathematics team. In preparation for the county-wide mathematics competition, we practiced after school for several weeks. On the day of the competition, I was nervous, excited, and determined to please Ms. Brown. I worked carefully on each problem. Much to my honest surprise, I was awarded the first-place prize in the county. To this day I have both the award and a copy of the competition's test in my scrapbook. I credit Ms. Brown's enthusiasm and that mathematics competition with helping to fuel in me the drive, the desire, and the dedicated passion for exploring and enjoying mathematics that has since been so much a part of my life.

In eighth grade, I enrolled in Algebra I and had a teacher named Miss Dickey. Miss Dickey was a happy, enthusiastic teacher who taught me some excellent habits. She encouraged writing in the mathematics classroom and required that all students maintain journals, which she collected periodically in order to read and respond to what students had written. Since then I have valued the integration of writing and mathematics; if people are able to explain their mathematical reasoning in writing, there is evidence that they have, indeed, learned deeply. Miss Dickey also valued technology. Although home computers were not yet popular when I was an eighth-grader, Miss Dickey had a vision of how crucial technology would be in the future. She encouraged meaningful, appropriate uses of calculators. She also took several of us on a field trip to Atlanta, where we visited Georgia Tech and heard professors discuss how technology was being used in college-level science and mathematics classrooms. I will never forget seeing the electron microscope; the professor who was demonstrating it showed a fly magnified thousands of times its original size. He explained the revolutionary nature of the electron microscope and hypothesized how it would lead to rich discoveries in both mathematics and science.

Ninth grade was an unusual year for me in the mathematics classroom. The class was geometry and the teacher was Mr. Castle. I believe that Mr. Castle was a first-year teacher who was pursuing a second or third career. He knew geometry well, and he was effective at explaining difficult concepts. Mr. Castle was even skillful in teaching us to write proofs, which many mathematics teachers consider to be one of the most difficult skills to teach. However, this geometry teacher definitely had his own way of doing things. He often called on students to teach segments of the lesson. Although I remember being nervous when having to stand in front of the class, I was also secretly delighted when it was my turn to teach. I found a special type of enjoyment in teaching, just as I had years earlier when I "taught" my stuffed animals. Another aspect of Mr. Castle's teaching that was different from anything I had previously experienced was that he would not allow us to earn an "A" on a test unless one of our parents came to visit the class for at least one entire class period. Extremely grade conscious, I made sure that my mother visited the classroom on several occasions. Furthermore, Mr. Castle felt that desks were distracting to us as students, so for several weeks, we were not allowed to use our desks. We had to sit in chairs, holding our materials and taking notes on our laps. I don't know if this tactic improved our attention, but it certainly made an imprint on my memory. I believe that was the only year that Mr. Castle taught mathematics—at least at my school. During the next academic year, he opened a store known as Comics Castle; the store sold comic books and fantasy games and was quite popular for a while.

By the end of ninth grade, I was definitely what one might call a mathematics enthusiast. I enjoyed learning and exploring mathematics. I found pleasure in the logic of applying rules and theorems. I often thought of mathematics problems as engaging puzzles or brain teasers. I never complained about mathematics, as did so many of my fellow students. I also began to think seriously about my future. I thought about teaching. I wondered if I could be like Mrs. Keller, my third-grade teacher, who knew how to design games and learning activities that made mathematics engaging and fun. I wondered if I could be like my seventh-grade teacher, Ms. Brown, whose enthusiasm for her area of expertise was definitely inspiring. I wondered if I might be able to make use of the teaching methods employed by my eighth-grade Algebra I teacher, Miss Dickey, who knew the value of integrating mathematics and communication and was exceptionally excited about technology. I wondered if I might, in some ways, be like Mr. Castle who, despite his unorthodox teaching methods, truly had a gift for explaining difficult concepts. I was fast approaching high school, which at that time began with tenth grade, and little did I know that when it came to mathematics teachers, the absolute best was yet to come.

On the first day of tenth grade, I was introduced to Mrs. Margaret Faircloth in a class called Algebra II and Trigonometry. I immediately knew she looked familiar. I had seen her picture in the newspaper a year or two earlier when she had been named teacher of the year for the county. She would become the most important and inspiring mentor I have ever known. I vividly remember our homework assignment on the first night of class Mrs. Faircloth gave us the following problem to solve: "A farmer has $100.00 and wants to buy 100 animals. Cows cost $10.00 each. Pigs cost $5.00 each. Chickens cost $.50 each. If the farmer must spend exactly $100.00 and must purchase exactly 100 animals, how many of each animal must the farmer purchase?" I remember working diligently on the problem that evening. I was able to come up with the solution (1 cow, 9 pigs, and 90 chickens) using trial and error, but I wanted to solve the problem with algebra. I suppose I worked for two hours or more, trying every algebraic configuration my mind could discover. In class the next day, I explained to Mrs. Faircloth that I knew the answer to the problem but that I had been unable to find the answer with algebra. She explained to me very kindly and patiently that there was not enough information given in the problem to solve it using algebra. There were three unknowns, but only two equations could be developed. I learned then—and never forgot—that an in order to be solved, an algebraic system of equations must contain the same number of equations as there are variables. As I write this chapter, I have been teaching for nearly fifteen years, and I have given that very same "farmer" problem to many of my students. It is a wonderful problem for teaching not only algebraic principles but also the importance of the problem solving process and the value of reflecting upon one's work.

The experience with the farmer problem may be the first memory I have related to Mrs. Faircloth's teaching, but it is only the first of many. I was fortunate enough to be Mrs. Faircloth's student not only in tenth grade, but also in eleventh grade (for Analysis) and in twelfth grade (for Advanced Placement Calculus). The three years I spent as Mrs. Faircloth's student shaped my life in wonderful ways that I am still realizing. I learned meaningful and rich lessons from this inspirational teacher. First of all, I gained knowledge in effective ways to teach. Mrs. Faircloth was tireless in her efforts to encourage her students to think. She knew how to ask thought-provoking questions that would "tease" our brains. She connected the mathematics concepts we discussed to other academic subjects and to life outside of school. She assessed our knowledge and understanding continually, and through a variety of assignments. Yes, Mrs. Faircloth gave tests and quizzes. Any student of hers will always remember her signature announcement preceding a surprise quiz, "Now I would like for you to have a clean desk, paper, and pencil." My heart would sink for just a few seconds when I would hear this. I don't know why. Mrs. Faircloth always taught concepts so masterfully that I should not have been afraid of the quizzes. This remarkable teacher also made use of more progressive means of assessment, including co-operative problem-solving exercises, performance assessments, and mathematics projects. I clearly remember the project I researched and constructed in tenth grade. I made a clay model of Stonehenge and wrote a report on the mathematics concepts theorized to have been connected with Stonehenge when it was built in ancient times. It was certainly a rich learning experience; I am still amazed when I view a television program or read a new piece of research related to Stonehenge. Mrs. Faircloth also taught us to use scientific calculators and valued the usefulness of technology. In her classroom, she nurtured a climate in which risk-taking was appreciated and where it was perfectly acceptable to make mistakes. Mrs. Faircloth made sure that her students realized that mistakes are a natural part of the learning process.

During my senior year of college, I was fortunate enough to be placed with Mrs. Faircloth for my student-teaching experience. Of course, I already knew what a masterful teacher she was. Being her student teacher allowed me to work with her as a colleague. What a tremendous opportunity for me! I quickly realized that being an excellent mathematics teacher means more than knowing mathematics content, and it means more than being able to teach the content to students. Indeed, it means being willing to collaborate with other teachers, with administrators, with parents of students, and with community members. It means knowing how to listen and not being afraid to share one's thoughts and opinions. It means finding value in hard work. (Without a doubt, Margaret Faircloth is one of the hardest workers I have ever known, and she does all of her work with a very willing spirit.) Excellence in mathematics teaching also means always having a positive attitude—toward mathematics, toward students, toward colleagues, and toward the everyday "nitty gritty" of teaching. Furthermore, the most wonderful teachers are those who view themselves as lifelong learners, always willing to grow and change, always honoring the importance of professional and personal transformation. Mrs. Faircloth is the epitome of a lifelong learner. Technically, she is now retired, after nearly forty years of teaching and educational leadership. I had the extreme pleasure of serving as the master of ceremonies at her retirement banquet. However, she stays busy constantly—planning and teaching professional development sessions to teachers throughout the state, serving as an adjunct instructor at several colleges, meaningfully interacting with other mathematics educators, and attending a variety of mathematics conferences.

Indeed, Mrs. Faircloth was—and is—one of my greatest mentors. Certainly, I learned a tremendous amount about teaching from her. However, I also learned how to embody some of the most important characteristics that human beings should possess. Among these are patience, kindness, cheerfulness, and perseverance. Mrs. Faircloth is loved by all who know her. She is viewed with the utmost of respect and admiration. Fortunately, she and I have remained close through all the years that have passed since I completed my student teaching. She has followed my career very closely. I think she was more excited than I was when I completed my Doctor of Education degree at Georgia Southern University.

I taught for seven years at the elementary school level—four years in kindergarten and three years in second grade. It was such a pleasure to observe young learners as they were blossoming. Teaching in self-contained classrooms gave me rich and wonderful opportunities to infuse mathematics within a variety of academic subjects and activities. Knowing that mathematics is often viewed as a "bad guy" in our society, I worked diligently to dispel the myth that mathematics is unimaginative and dull. Although I have lost touch with many of my students from my years of elementary school teaching, I definitely pray that those students have strengthened their appreciation of mathematics as they have gotten older.

As a two-time Mercer University alumnus (Bachelor of Arts in Mathematics, 1989, and Education Specialist in Early Childhood Education, 1995), I was delighted when I was given the opportunity to return to Mercer as an instructor. Currently in my eighth year of teaching mathematics education courses, I have interacted with and taught hundreds of pre-service and in-service teachers. I find marvelous pleasure in my work—every single day. I find excitement in planning and implementing learning activities for my students, whom I lovingly encourage to have positive attitudes toward mathematics—and to spread these positive attitudes to their students. Certainly, many of my students, as well as many people throughout society have unfavorable memories associated with mathematics teachers and classes. I explain that those unfavorable memories can serve as inspiration—inspiration to ensure that today's youngsters do not grow up with similar unfavorable memories. "We are the change agents," I tell my adult students. "We are the teachers who must do all that we can to let people know that mathematics is exciting, fresh, engaging, and fun. We must attempt to do away with the notion that it is acceptable to perform poorly in mathematics. We must build students' confidence and competence in mathematics."

Tennyson believed that "we are a part of all we have met." The older I become, the more I believe this, as well. Within my being, within my soul, and within my heart are bits and pieces of the personalities of all those who have influenced me over the years. Indeed, Mrs. Faircloth's influence shines forth in every lesson that I teach. When I show patience and kindness to my students, when I ask questions that stimulate thinking, when I assess my students' learning through a variety of methods, when I connect mathematics to life outside of the classroom, and when I find pleasure in being a lifelong learner, I am a reflection, at least to some degree, of Margaret Faircloth. I know that I owe more to her than even I can realize. Certainly, however, others have affected the teacher that I have become. My mother and father spent hours helping me with homework and encouraging me to do my best. My grandmother taught me mathematics and other subjects through games—Candy Land when I was younger, and Scrabble and Trivial Pursuit when I was older. All other teachers of mine, including those mentioned earlier, have left their influence on me as well. I was taught by many enthusiastic and effective professors during my fourteen years of higher education; I know that I emulate a number of these women and men when I teach. Even those teachers of mine who were not considered favorites have helped me to know what *not* to do in the classroom. Indeed, when I teach, I express my humanness—a humanness that has been shaped by all who have affected me throughout my life. Just as I have been touched by many others, I find delight in knowing that I might touch others through my teaching. I also hope that my students, who are or will be teachers, find pleasure in knowing that they have opportunities to touch unknown numbers of lives. As stated beautifully by Albert Einstein, "Setting an example is not the main means of influencing another; it is the only means." I am heartened in knowing that I might serve as a positive example to others, just as so many have served as positive examples to me. As I continue my career in the field of education, I continue to pursue my passion, my calling, my joy in life. Indeed, every new day in the classroom confirms my sincere belief that I was born to teach.

Remembering Ruby

Linda Adams, Ed.D.

When I was a child, my favorite cousin was a teacher. She was well respected in the community, and everyone seemed to treat her as if she had special powers. I really didn't know why people were drawn to her. She seemed to have a type of magical persona that people just loved. From the time that I met her, I knew that I wanted to be like her. I wanted to look like her, dress like her, and emulate her personality. I wanted to copy every move she made. She and my mother were very good friends. Therefore, my cousin visited us often. Her name was Mrs. Williams, but my mother and grandmother addressed her by her first name, Ruby. She always treated us kids warmly during her visits. However, most of her time was spent with the grown ups. Very little attention or time was given to us. That didn't bother me much because just getting a glimpse of her was enough for me. I used to ask my mother endless questions about her. Through her answers I learned that the special powers and the magical persona that Mrs. Williams possessed were due to the fact that she was a teacher. I knew right then and there that I was going to become a teacher. Whenever my sister Flossie, my cousin Gloria, and the neighborhood kids played, I always wanted to play school, so I could be the teacher.

Sometimes they would let me play this game, but I was the youngest of the bunch and usually had to follow their lead. Whenever they let me play school, I would always be Mrs. Williams. I insisted that all the kids playing the game call me Mrs. Williams. They would not let me play the game for long, but that didn't bother me. Even if they let me play the game for only a few minutes, the experience of pretending to be Mrs. Williams was the highlight of my day.

My fascination with my favorite cousin increased as I grew older. My second year of school was a "hurry up and get through" year. I couldn't wait to get to the third grade because I knew that Mrs. Williams was going to be my teacher. The first day in her class was like heaven. She was even warmer, kinder, more nurturing, and more loving than I had experienced previously. She treated all of her students the same. We were all poor when it came to material things, but Mrs. Williams cultivated richness in our souls that made us overlook the holes in our shoes and the greasy bag lunches that we carried so proudly to school each day. Being a student in her class made me want to be the same kind of caring, nurturing teacher when I grew up. I remember how patient she was with me when I couldn't quite get a concept that she was teaching. She would always say, "Linda, I will help you to learn this." She would take her soft and ever so caring hands and wipe my tears away. Then she would look at me with a caring smile and say, "Don't cry. Sometimes it takes a little more time to learn certain things. Let's stop for now and kick this cow again tomorrow. Who knows; she just may get up and run." Mrs. Williams was funny like that. She always made you feel as if you were very special to her, even though she had more than thirty other students in her class. After she finished assuring me that everything was going to be all right, I would smile at her request. Then she would wrap her soft arms around me and give me that much needed hug. Soon the fear of learning the new concept would fade away, and I would be off to enjoy another facet of learning in the classroom.

The next day, Mrs. Williams and I would pull the old cow out again to see if we could make her move. Sometimes we would kick that cow for several days or even a week before she would get up and run. But one thing was for sure, Mrs. Williams, my trusting and kind teacher, was always there by my side until that cow got up and ran. Just being in her class made my life take on new meaning. I felt that there wasn't anything that I couldn't do. More importantly, she taught me, through her funny antics, that you can accomplish any goal if you are patient and persistent in your approach. I also learned from Mrs. Williams that, in some odd way, all cows are the same and they can be made to move and even run.

One day after school, I asked Mrs. Williams, "How do you become a teacher?" I will never forget her answer. She chuckled and said, "My child, it is a gift to be a teacher. Not everyone can be a teacher. You have to study hard, but teaching does not come from the books you study. They only give you the knowledge to teach. Becoming a teacher comes from the soul and the heart." This statement made absolutely no sense to me at the time. Instead, I began to view teaching as this impossible task that I would never be able to accomplish. I didn't have the gift, nor did I have any idea of where to find it. I often wondered who gave the gift to her and why she couldn't pass it on to me. At that point, I made up in my mind that before I left her class, I was going to ask her if she could either give me this gift or tell me where I could find it. Then, reality sank in. I thought to myself, "If I find the gift, I will probably have to buy it." I was a child. I didn't have any money to buy a gift. Discouraged at the thought of being unable to purchase the gift, I began to think that my dream of becoming a teacher was done and gone. I tried to set my sights on becoming something else, but the idea of becoming a teacher would not go away. I often thought about the gift but did not speak of it again to Mrs. Williams until I was much older. One day during my sophomore year of high school, she visited my mother. During her visit, she came over and sat beside me and put her warm, loving arms around me. With a big smile she asked, "How is my little teacher today?" I looked at her with surprise in my eyes because I thought that she had long forgotten that I told her that I wanted to be a teacher when I was in her third-grade class. She continued her conversation by saying, "You are going to be a fine teacher one day because you are kind, caring, and concerned about others." Then, to my surprise, Mrs. Williams said, "How would *you* like to help me teach my Sunday school class this coming Sunday? You can be my little teacher helper." My mother was standing nearby smiling with pride. I was excited and scared at the same time. In one second, I thought to myself, "What an honor to work with her." Then, in the next second, I thought, "I can't do this. I don't have the 'gift.'" Somehow the second thought came rolling out of my mouth. I could hear myself say to her, "But I don't have the gift to teach." Mrs. Williams only laughed a hearty laugh, hugged me tightly, and said, "I guess I will just have to help you to find it." Later that day when I thought about the events of our conversation, it dawned on me that we—Mrs. Williams, my favorite cousin, my admired third-grade teacher, and I—had just kicked another cow and made her run.

After several months of helping Mrs. Williams with her Sunday school class, I learned that the gift was a strong desire to help others grow and learn at their maximum potential. I also learned that you have to take a personal interest in the learning of each of the students in your class because not all students learn in the same manner. She taught me that you get to know how each child learns and that you gear your teaching to his or her ability. Lastly, I began to understand what she meant when she said that teaching comes from the soul and the heart. There is something inside of you that makes you want to touch the heart and soul of every student you teach. It has no name. You can't even begin to describe it. But you know that "it," whatever it is, is right there inside of you.

Today as I look back at my experiences and interactions with Mrs. Williams, I can truly say that she was a "teacher" before her time. She wasn't a scholar of individualized instruction, cooperative learning, direct/indirect instructional strategies, or self-directed learning. Nor was she well versed on the various types of tools used to assess the learner's performance. In her day, there was no such thing as "portfolio development." Neither did she know about questioning strategies or even how to develop goals and objectives to create developmentally appropriate lesson plans for her students. But somehow she did it all under the auspices of what she termed, "good teaching." Mrs. Williams was what we would classify today as an effective "master teacher." Little did I know that my fascination with this wonderful character of a woman at a very early age in my life would have such a dynamic impact, not only on what I would become in life, but also on how I would structure my teaching as a professional educator.

Some thirty years ago, I found the "gift" of teaching in Mrs. Ruby Williams' Sunday school class. Today, the act of teaching has become much more cultivated, but the underlying passion of it all is still the same. No two teachers are alike. Each starts out on a journey searching for that special gift that will make him or her exceptional in the field. What each will find is that the journey is never-ending and that he or she will evolve and transform many times before the classroom doors close. As an Associate Professor in the Tift College of Education at Mercer University, I find new vigor with each course I teach. I have learned so much over the years about the process of teaching. The principles that I hold sacred to my heart are those that inspire others who have the desire to teach and to cultivate a love affair with the profession. I tell my pre-service teachers that they will learn much tangible knowledge in their coursework and through their field experiences, but the "inner gift" of becoming a teacher includes those intangible ventures such as patience, compassion, a nurturing spirit, and, above all, love for the students that they will someday teach and inspire on a daily basis.

As I look back through the chronicle of my teaching, Mrs. Williams has been with me every step of the way. Unknown to her or to me, she has guided my steps in the teaching profession from her third-grade class to where I am today. I can truly say I have found the gift of teaching, and, with each course I teach, I try to pass on a little of that gift to the pre-service teachers who are also searching for that burning passion to teach. I still have challenges that I am working on as a teacher. And I figure there will always be one or two or even three that I will have to deal with until the day I retire from the field. But each time a new or even an old challenge appears, I still remember the strategy that Mrs. Williams taught me in her third-grade class, "Kick the cow until she moves." This chapter was written with fond memories of my favorite cousin, my third-grade teacher, my mentor and friend, Mrs. Ruby Williams.

Stand

Penny L Elkins, Ph.D.

I recently read an anonymous quote that said, "We will be judged in this life by two things: what we stand for and what we fall for." There are many things for which we stand in our lives—our values, our beliefs, our convictions, our faith, and our families. As important as these foundational principles are, we must also make decisions every day about those things for which we won't fall.

My passion for teaching begins here....with those things for which I simply won't fall. I don't allow myself or my students to fall for untruths that undermine success.

The first of these false statements is "one person cannot make a difference." We cannot allow ourselves to devalue the importance and significance of one human being in the life of another.

I never wanted to be a teacher. For those who know my current passion for teaching, this statement might be difficult to believe. I respected and loved all of my teachers and saw the tremendous significance they made in my life, but I simply had no desire to teach. I graduated as the valedictorian of my high school class and became the first person in my family to graduate from college. I was captain of the debate team and went to Mercer University on a Jesse Mercer scholarship with the full intention of majoring in political science and then going to Mercer's prestigious law school.

That was my plan until I met Dr. Bobby Jones, an education professor who taught me "foundations of education," an elective course that I chose to take in my second year at Mercer. I took the course only because I could not find another course that would fit into my schedule.

One semester with Bobby would change my life forever. He ignited within me what was already there: a passion to teach. He showed me that one person can inspire and empower a single individual—or even a large group of individuals—not necessarily by what that person says but by how he acts. I knew when Dr. Bobby walked into class that he had complete and total conviction about his passion for education. He knew that the only way for others to be successful was to continue learning. Education was the key to the future for him and he modeled it consistently for us. His attitude inspired me and others to want to teach.

The passion that was instilled within me has only intensified over time, and for that I have Bobby, and many other people who came after Bobby, to thank.

One person does make a difference. Bobby Jones was that person for me and every day I challenge myself to be a "Dr. Bobby" for others.

We can't ever fall for thinking that one person cannot significantly alter the course of another's life.

Settling for mediocrity—having low expectations for ourselves and for others—is the second point for which I encourage others never to fall. Aristotle once said, "Excellence is a habit, not an act," meaning that we must strive continuously for quality. It is not just a one-time event.

From the time I was a very young girl, my father instilled within me two things: work ethic and excellence. My sisters and I were never allowed to settle for less than our best effort. In my family, we were encouraged to strive for excellence, not perfection. We understood that we were all very unique and had different talents, but we were expected to use those talents for the betterment of ourselves and others around us.

I am always humbled when I think of how I have been blessed in my life because of those values. I graduated from Mercer, taught for three years while at the same time getting my master's degree in early childhood education first and then in educational leadership, became an elementary school administrator at the age of twenty-five, earned my doctorate by the time I was twenty-nine years old and now have been a college professor for ten years, eight of which have been as department chair. Interestingly, I never applied for a position. I simply did my work with excellence and the path appeared before me. I never accept mediocrity nor will I allow my students to do so.

My research interests focus on brain theory and leadership. When I study the brain and its incredible potential, I am reminded that often we underestimate the capacity of the individual. There is so much more that can be learned, embraced, and experienced in this life. I want my students to leave the classroom with a thirst for knowledge, a love for learning new ideas, and a commitment to inspire their students to do the same.

Whatever I challenge my students to accomplish, I never let them settle for mediocrity, no matter what their socioeconomic background or educational exceptionalities.

We can't ever fall for believing that mediocrity is the acceptable norm.

The final belief for which I encourage myself and others never to fall is that negativity is a part of life. Negativity is a trap that slowly permeates the fabric of our being. There will always be people around us who will not celebrate our achievements. A friend of mine often says, "If people try to steal your dreams, it just means that they don't have any of their own." We will encounter people (even teachers and school leaders) who will say, "We have to do it this way because we always have."

We just can't fall for it.

We will hear others say, "Those children can't learn. Look at their backgrounds."

We just can't fall for it.

The test is to remain positive when others are not. The test is to believe when others don't and to inspire when others are defeated. It has been said that even the most positive of individuals—if surrounded by negativity—will become negative over time.

We simply can't fall for negativity.

For teachers this means that we will at times be the ones who will have to take stands for our students when others won't. It is the job of those who aspire to teach to challenge the status quo respectfully for the betterment of students. We've all had teachers who took stands for us. I believe it is my job to take stands for students and more importantly, to empower my students to take stands for themselves.

So, why do I teach? I teach for all of the students who have taught me the importance of taking stands for them.

I teach for Rico, who taught me that I was not the only person in the room who could teach Kenneth how to subtract across zeroes. It was Rico who taught Kenneth in three minutes what I had tried to for three weeks. Rico taught me that we are a community of learners, each a valuable member of the community, none more important than the other.

I teach for Michael, a child who by his own admission had little to be excited about in life, until we decided to hatch chickens in third grade. It was Michael who was so inspired by observing and analyzing data on chickens that he went on to become a research scientist. Michael taught me that one learning activity can determine the course of a student's life.

Or what about Jernetta? Jernetta taught me that quiet children have a lot to say. She never spoke much in class until I gave an open-ended assignment in poetry writing. I told the students they could present their poems to the class in a manner in which they preferred. It was my quiet Jernetta who taught us all how to rap before rap was popular! Jernetta taught me never to underestimate the potential of each individual.

I teach for Sonya, who taught me the power of love. Sonya believed that no matter how tough the children, she could teach them with love. In college, I taught her how to be a good teacher, and she reminded me how to love children until one could teach them. Her persistence on behalf of children inspired me to want to do more. Sonya taught me to remember that those who sit before me in class are people first, then students.

I continue to take stands for students every day. I expect them to believe that they make a difference. I expect them never to settle for mediocrity but to embrace excellence. I expect them to see the best in others and themselves. I just won't allow them—or myself—to fall for any less.

Teaching:
A Cross-Cultural Passion

Ismail Simbwa Gyagenda, Ph.D.

My desire to teach goes back to my elementary and high school years in Uganda in the 1960s and 1970s. I had some incredibly passionate teachers whose enthusiasm for the profession was contagious and who left an indelible mark on my psyche. Before I share my teaching experiences in the graduate classrooms at Mercer and discuss the philosophy that undergirds my teaching, I cannot help but reminisce about the memories of those teachers who, during my most impressionable period, engendered in me the love for teaching. When the time came for selecting a college major (in Uganda, this was done during the college application process in the last year of high school), I had no qualms whatsoever about choosing education, although it was an unpopular choice among my peers who fancied law, business, medicine, engineering, and political science. I have never regretted my decision. It is interesting to note that some of my graduate students here at Mercer, like my peers in Uganda more than twenty years ago, rejected education as their college major, only to change their minds after becoming disenchanted with their careers in corporate

America. I am glad I have, for so long been doing what I love, thanks partly to the amazing teachers in my past.

I remember vividly my math teacher in the third grade, Mr. Isaac Magezi, who taught with such gusto and cheerfulness that we all could hardly wait for his class time. Later on, he became our headmaster (principal) and again our math teacher in grade seven, the last year of the elementary cycle in Uganda. By that time, math, especially algebra, was starting to become a chore for me and for the majority in my class. Yet, we were busy preparing for the high-stakes national Primary Leaving Examination (PLE), on which one had to score at a high level to get into a prestigious government high school. Thanks to Mr. Magezi, who rejected our claims that we were "allergic" to algebraic formulae, I came to terms with math. Using drama, humor, and ordinary examples, he pushed us, on a daily basis, to try out as many math problems as possible. I scored very well on that high-stakes exam and was accepted at Mbarara High School, one of the best high schools in the country at that time. With very few vacancies in reputable government boarding high schools, education was so competitive at the time that I shudder to think what would have happened to me if I had failed that exam.

I enrolled in the high school in 1970, and there I met other wonderful teachers who became inspirational in my journey to the profession I cherish. One teacher stands out in my high school years. Ralph Elwell-Sutton, a Scottish World War II Major, was a teacher in his late fifties. He taught English Language (a compulsory subject) and Literature in English (an elective subject). At the end of the ninth grade, we had to choose between literature and religious studies for our national high school exams due at the end of the eleventh grade. Because literature was considered to be more difficult than religious studies and past exam statistics indicated this fact, most students in my class (about twenty-five out of thirty-six) opted for religious studies. To ensure that the two options had an equal number of students, Mr. Sutton encouraged us to persuade more students to enroll into the literature class. He concluded by declaring, "I guarantee that if you opt for literature, you will pass the National Literature Exam at the end of your high school career." No teacher had ever made that kind of assertion. The confidence and forcefulness with which he spoke convinced seven more students, albeit reluctantly, to cross over to the literature group. For the next two years, Mr. Sutton turned all of us into little masters of the English language. Through targeted homework, detailed feedback on assignments, dramatization, humor, constant practice on grammar and mechanics, oral reading, etc., Major Elwell-Sutton made us realize our potential in the two subjects. What mostly stood out in his teaching was the utter passion and devotion that he exuded. He had our attention from the moment he entered class; he was always prepared; he quickly knew us by name; he came to know each students' weaknesses and strengths; he encouraged us, counseled us, and challenged us. The high expectations implied in his "guarantee" were daily demonstrated in the way he engaged us in the classroom. No wonder then that when the results from the 1973 High School Exam came back, all of us had passed the literature exam with flying colors. I strongly believe that the indelible impact of Major Sutton and other exemplary teachers in my youth not only steered me subconsciously into the education profession, but probably influenced my philosophy of, and attitude towards, teaching.

To describe and discuss my passion for teaching may seem vain, from a Ugandan cultural perspective. In my Ganda culture (the Ganda or Baganda is the largest tribe in Uganda), personal expressions of "passion," romantic or otherwise, are uncommon except in poetry and music. The rationale behind this cultural norm is that if you indeed have a passion for something, you show it in action, and those around you witness it, rather than hearing you talking or bragging about that passion. However, I am comfortable sharing my passion for teaching, without fearing that I will offend my cultural spirits because of the potential benefits this discussion may have for the profession.

Teaching is exciting to me in all its complex facets. Irvine articulates so eloquently the following "essential elements" of teaching: "1. some person, 2. teaching something, 3. to some student, 4. somewhere."[1] Using these elements as an anchor for discussing my passion for teaching, I will now share my philosophy, the method(s) and approach(es) I employ in teaching the various courses at Mercer, my perception of the graduate students I teach (what I enjoy in engaging them, what I expect of them, how I interact with them), and finally, my understanding of the place I teach: Tift College of Education, Mercer University.

The first element "some person" refers to the teacher. It has been said that "we teach who we are."[2] My philosophy of

---

[1] J. J. Irvine, *Educating Teachers for Diversity: Seeing with a Cultural Eye* (New York: Teachers College Press 2003) 45.

[2] Parker J. Palmer, *The Courage to Teach: Exploring the Inner Landscape of a Teacher's Life* (San Francisco CA: Jossey-Bass Publishers 1998) 1.

teaching indeed is influenced by who I am. Various descriptors apply to me: male, black, African (Ugandan in particular), middle-aged, Muslim, half liberal, half conservative, doctor of philosophy. It is difficult to discern which of the above descriptors have largely influenced my philosophy of teaching, but I do have strong beliefs on what my role as a professor in a graduate teacher program should be. I see my role as challenging my students to think critically about what they are learning and about what they are or will be doing in their classrooms. I must continually raise questions to probe their perceptions of schooling and how they see their role in the field. I strongly believe that schools have a responsibility to ensure that all students, irrespective of their backgrounds, are challenged to reach their potential. I also strongly believe in being open-minded: I am willing and eager to listen and learn from others, including my students. The passion with which I hold these beliefs may not be easily visualized or discerned by others. However, it manifests itself in the method and approach I employ in the graduate courses I teach at Mercer.

The second element of teaching "teaching something" is about the subject(s) or course(s) one teaches. To illustrate the joyful passion I find in teaching, I will use examples from two of the courses I teach: Educational Research, and Culturally Responsive Pedagogy. It is interesting that many of my students come with distorted preconceived notions about both courses. With regard to Educational Research, they are apprehensive about statistics because they think the two are synonymous. Regarding Culturally Responsive Pedagogy, they are not only intimidated by the title of the course, but they seem to have a socialized reluctance to discuss things cultural. My work is therefore cut out for me, so to say.

In Educational Research, I intentionally focus on the students' ability to understand the concepts of the research process. Using familiar examples from the schools, we come to appreciate the notion of research methodology as "disciplined inquiry,"[3] the logical steps of the scientific method, and the relevance of qualitative methodology in trying to understand complex social contexts. For example, regarding the problem of potential researcher bias, I use a basketball match scenario. Imagine you are the coach for your high school basketball team. You have reached the finals. You lead your team to the final's venue. At the last minute, the referee fails to turn up. Officials of the tournament discuss the problem and decide to select you as the referee of the game. Are you going to be a biased or a neutral referee? Naturally, you support your team, but you have a professional and moral responsibility to remain neutral as a referee. In fact, the validity and acceptability of the results at the end of that game are dependent on your objectivity and neutrality as a referee, as witnessed by the audience. Likewise, the validity of the research results depends on the objectivity and neutrality of the researcher. However much the researcher may support a certain hypothesis, once the experiment begins, he or she must remain neutral and let the chips fall where they may. Once the research community is convinced of that neutrality, the validity of the results will be enhanced and vice versa.

---

[3] L. S. Shulman, "Disciplines of Inquiry in Education: An Overview," *Educational Researcher* 10/6 (1981): 5–12, 23.

Using such examples, my students soon come to realize that the research process is more about logic, objectivity, transparency, and common sense than statistics. They are led to think like researchers about narrowing down research questions, choosing appropriate methods, good sampling, and the rationale behind literature reviews. Before long, with their initial fear somewhat diminished, they are demanding to do the statistical equations to help them answer their research questions. How exhilarating it is for me as I witness this transformation!

In the Culturally Responsive Pedagogy class, the students are expected to engage in "cultural immersion experiences" (CIE), a practice started by my former colleague, Ms. Beth Allgood-McCkinnon. Students are required to visit a minority family and attend at least three minority cultural events such as weddings, festivals, and religious sites/festivities. They then report their experiences to the whole class and we discuss what they learned and gained. In the fall semester of 2004, two of my students were so apprehensive about visiting a different culture that they e-mailed me, requesting to opt out of that particular assignment. In our next class meeting, I explained to the whole class that the rationale behind these experiences was to help teachers overcome such fears, as well as to help them to interact in real life contexts with the diverse cultures represented in their classrooms. Despite the initial trepidation, the reports at the end of the semester were incredible, with all students indicating how much they had learned from the experiences: stereotypes were debunked, new perspectives on the home environment of different cultural groups were gained, and appreciation of the different cultures improved. Teachers who informed some of their students about visiting the events reported how the students' morale and motivation increased tremendously. The relevance of this course was very much validated by these assignments, and the vast majority of students who take this class finish it with a strong appreciation for the need to integrate culturally responsive pedagogy into their practice. The student teachers acknowledge that it is very easy to monopolize their teaching with mainstream examples and sources of reference. The class forces them to think differently, to search for ways of introducing other cultural referents and sources into their repertoire, thereby truly acknowledging the worth and essence of the minority groups in their classrooms. By the end of the semester, I am always amazed how changed the students are. Although as a foreigner, I may harbor a bias for the subject, it is gratifying to observe continually the students' gradual transformation from timid and reluctant stances at the beginning of the semester to animated discussants of cultures and how their infusion into daily classroom activities is beneficial for all.

The third element in teaching, "to some student," demands that I need to know my students. What perceptions do I have of these students, their strengths, weaknesses, and potential? What do I hope to accomplish with them? My students are mostly American, almost equal ratio of White and African American plus a small number of other ethnic groups, mostly female, mostly above twenty-five years old. They are intelligent, and they know what they want at Mercer: to get certified as teachers or to get graduate degrees in teaching. The former group comes from different academic and career backgrounds. They exhibit a variety of strengths and weaknesses typical in similar graduate programs. As to their potential, my assumption is that the sky is the limit. As I interact with them, I see my role as that of challenging them at a philosophical and academic level. I don't want them to take teaching for granted. In the school philosophy course that I teach, they must articulate their vision and what they see as their role in the classroom. It is not enough to describe Plato's ideas about education and morality. My students must reflect and articulate their own notion of morality in today's schools. They must also research what current philosophers opine on these issues. At the beginning of each philosophy class, we talk about current events, dealing with schools and education in general. School philosophy, as far as I am concerned, is not an esoteric discussion of what the "ancients" and the "moderns" thought or think about schools. Rather, teachers must read those sources, be able to reflect critically on current practices and policies in public schools, and be able to think about how these practices and policies may be shaped by certain competing, if not contradictory, philosophical underpinnings. Finally, the teachers must ask: so what is my role, given all this "philosophical musing"? To these teachers, I strongly assert that they have enormous power, in spite of the sometimes disabling external forces they may perceive. They must never forget their ultimate power to make a difference in the lives of the children they face when they close the classroom door. Their focus and energy must be to that "captive audience." Should they allow themselves to be distracted by negative voices from outside, be it immediate administrators, the school board, or the politicians, then they will be caught in that impossible dilemma of trying to serve two masters, and it is the children who will lose. I often quote them the Ugandan proverb, "When elephants fight, it is the grass that suffers." If I did not sincerely believe in teachers' power and positive influence in children's lives, I probably would choose a career other than one at the Tift College of Education, Mercer University.

The fourth and last element of teaching, "somewhere," refers to where one is teaching. What are my perceptions about Mercer University, especially the Tift College of Education? One's passion for teaching or for any other vocation can be enabled or stifled by the work environment. I count as one of my many blessings the fact that the Tift College of Education puts a premium on teaching. The college's mission, as captured in its conceptual framework, "To Know, To Do, To Be," envisions teachers as transformers. My philosophy tallies with this holistic approach to teacher preparation. The enabling environment at Mercer allows me to interact with my students, to hear their stories, to challenge them to reflect on their praxis, to learn from them about the children they teach, and, with them, to seek better ways of realizing the potential of these children. We, at the Tift College of Education, share the notion that the children must be our primary priority, and our task is to prepare teachers who never lose sight of that focus.

It is my sincere hope that I can recreate in my students the joyful cross-cultural passion and commitment to teaching exemplified by the wonderful teachers in my youth like Mr. Magezi, who hailed from rural Uganda, and like Major Elwell-Sutton from Scotland. I also hope that my students will continually and critically reflect on the multifaceted nature of teaching, someone teaching something to some student somewhere, with the aim of defining for themselves the critical role they have to play in that complex continuum.

Full Circle

Len Lancette, Ed.D.

Mary was clearly college material. A member of a large family in upstate New York, she had always earned good grades and she looked forward to attending college after high school. The family had lost one child to leukemia earlier, but seemed on the emotional mend during her senior year. Tragically, before her graduation, Mary's younger brother was murdered while witnessing an armed robbery at a convenience store. The family was traumatized by this event, and college for Mary faded into the background. She felt the need to escape that environment and moved away shortly after graduation. She began working, and she soon married and started a family. College was no longer an immediate goal. Fast-forward fifteen years and here is Mary enrolled in my class at Mercer University's Tift College of Education.

As a social studies specialist on the Tift College faculty, I've always been interested in the lives that people lead, not only historical figures who influenced the course of history, but also those people who are known only to a small circle of friends and family. Some of these are my students. How have their lives unfolded to the point that they are now seeking degrees from Mercer University? Why didn't they go directly to college after high school? Where have they been and what have they done? What significant events and circumstances have led them here? What choices have they made along the way, and what were the consequences of those decisions? Why have they decided to change the course of their personal histories at this juncture in their lives? Mary is one of many non-traditional students attending classes at Mercer University.

College students are generally classified as either traditional, those somewhat inexperienced eighteen- to twenty-year-old high school graduates venturing out on their own for the first time, and the non-traditional, typically experienced men and women returning to higher education after a lengthy absence. These are generally older students, usually over twenty-five years old, who did not follow the traditional route from high school to college. According to the National Center for Education Statistics, 11.7 percent of college students were in this category in 1980. By 2001, that percentage increased to 20.8 percent. Because of the "New Economy," or the "Knowledge Economy," or because of outsourcing or downsizing, that percentage continues to rise. And I am lucky to have these students in my classes. Being a Mercer University instructor is a wonderful profession. I have the opportunity to work along with people who are changing lives; those who are actually changing their own lives, and those who facilitate that journey. It is a joy to be a Tift College of Education faculty member who has the privilege of working with non-traditional students who bring such rich personal histories to the classroom.

The Tift College faculty is very good at working with non-traditional students. This is probably because of the faculty's shared commitment to teaching as our primary mission. We spend the majority of our time planning and preparing for classes, teaching classes, assessing, advising, and encouraging our non-traditional students. Unlike other universities that emphasize research and publishing over teaching, our energies are committed to teaching over research. To the Tift faculty, nothing is more important than teaching well so that our students can become good teachers themselves.

Who are these non-traditional students, and why do I feel fortunate to be able to teach these students? I teach in the Regional Academic Centers. In an introductory education class I taught recently, there were eighteen students. Sixteen were female. The youngest was twenty-three, the oldest forty-eight. Four were in their twenties, six in their thirties, and eight in their forties. The average age was thirty-six years, one month. In my experience at Mercer, this was not an atypical class. Each member of that class had decided that the time had come in life to shift gears. A convergence of circumstance and opportunity gave each a chance to pause and reassess. They reflected on their lives and decided to invest their time, money, and resources into driving in a new direction. They want to learn to become teachers. It is my good fortune to be able to assist them in this effort.

What is great about teaching these students is that they bring such rich and varied life experiences to the program. They've been around. They are not naive. They can't be fooled or flimflammed. They challenge us as teachers. This is one of the reasons we devote so much of our time to preparing and planning for our classes. These are wise consumers who know if they are getting their money's worth or not. And they've had enough life experience that they are not reluctant to let us know if they feel short-changed in any way. They challenge us to be good at what we do.

Why didn't they go directly to college after high school? Or if they did, why didn't they finish the first time through? Answers to these questions illustrate how rich their experiences have been. They've experienced both success and failure in their work lives and in their personal lives. They've had joy and they have had sadness. They have been very lucky, and very unlucky. But they are resilient. Whether born that way, or nurtured that way, they have survived and have committed to constructing the rest of their lives in a manner consistent with the lessons learned. I'll share a few of these stories.

Most of the students are women, so it is not unexpected that child-bearing often has delayed college attendance. Of the class mentioned above, eleven of the sixteen females are parents, most of them single parents. In these situations, giving birth and providing childcare prevented them from attending college earlier in life. Beyond this common experience, their stories diverge greatly. For example, one student had only earned a GED, while another had three and a half years at Georgia Tech. They are now classmates with the shared goal of becoming teachers.

Some came from families with high educational attainment, others did not. For example, Angela had a mother, grandmother, and aunts who were teachers with at least masters degrees. She graduated with honors from her middle and high schools, and attended a university in Virginia for one year. She even made the dean's list that year. But then she transferred to a university in Atlanta in order to be closer to her boyfriend. You can probably guess the rest of the story: the Buckhead nightlife, credit card consumer debt, a job, marriage, and children. She went to work in the corporate world, and would probably still be there except for the onset of a combination of serious health problems. This interruption in her life gave her the time to reflect on her life to that point, and imagine what she wanted the rest of her life to be like. Once she overcame her health problems, she decided to honor her heritage, complete her degree at Mercer, and become a teacher.

Mike, her classmate of about the same age also came from a family of high educational achievers. But in Mike's own words, "I was too smart for my own good." In a sort of passive-aggressive way, he chose to rebel against the family tradition and refused to enroll in college. Instead, he joined the Air Force where he served for seven years. He actually trained firemen to park fire trucks between cones without hitting them. Although the need for firemen who can parallel park their fire engines seems limited, he did enjoy his time as an instructor in the Air Force, and he would have remained except, like Angela, he also ran up against an obstacle. He became unable to meet the strict height/weight requirements of the Air Force and had to end his enlistment. Since then, this married father has been fairly successful in the corporate world, but he too came to realize that he cannot deny his heritage or his enjoyment of instructing, so he also enrolled at Mercer and will soon graduate as a certified middle school teacher.

Others don't come from family traditions that include college. Two members of the class earned GED certificates rather than high school diplomas. One got pregnant and married after tenth grade. In the rural community where she grew up, pregnant girls were discouraged from attending public school. Now that her own children have finished high school, she decided to "follow my original dream of becoming a teacher." The other student was attending a parochial high school and dropped out during her junior year for unspecified reasons. Over the years, she has picked up some college credit from institutions in three different states. Now, she has become settled and involved with her own children's schools. This involvement has inspired her to decide to complete her degree and become a teacher.

Some students were unable to attend college after high school due to financial reasons. For example, Craig's family moved to Georgia after he graduated from high school and would have had to pay out-of-state tuition. He decided to get a job while he established residence. His parents divorced during that period and consequently there were no family college funds available even after becoming a full-time resident. Over the years, Craig discovered a talent for tutoring children in math and decided to enroll in the Tift College of Education. With only a semester to go, he has achieved one of the highest GPAs in his class. Stacy is another student whose parents divorced about the time she was to graduate from high school, and she too was unable to finance further studies. Years later, she and Craig are in the same Tift College cohort and scheduled to graduate in the spring.

Tift College students have such fascinating histories. I could tell about the forty-year-old Navy brat who has been to so many places and done so many things; about the home-schooler whose experiences helped her realize that she should teach; about the one who floated through a series of jobs in the restaurant, retail, and medical fields unable to commit to anything until she began to volunteer in her daughter's school; or about how the demands of the insurance business took too much time from another mother's biological child and two adopted children.

I have to salute Kelly, whose boredom at a technical college convinced her she needed to work with people instead of programs. And I have to respect Shelly who was the "invisible" student in school, Kenna whose kindergarten teacher "diagnosed" her as mentally handicapped/ retarded (what an awful label for a child to carry through school), Meredith who was labeled a troublemaker in school, and Cynthia who did not score high enough on the SAT to be accepted at Georgia State twenty-eight years ago. Finally, I am so pleased to have Cora in my class. Neither of her parents graduated from high school, and although she was an honor student, there was little encouragement from her parents to go to college, and even less funding. She has toiled for thirteen years in the fast-food industry and worked her way up to assistant manager of a KFC. When her mother died recently, she reassessed her life and goals and decided she could do better. She is now carrying a 3.75 GPA at Mercer.

The transition from being in the working world or full-time parenting back to being a student is one more challenge that these students accept. Perhaps the biggest adjustment after years of establishing themselves in their current positions is that they are basically returning to entry-level status. They are choosing the unknown over the known. They choose financial sacrifice and many, many long evenings in the classroom and in study. There are difficult hurdles to overcome. Many worry that they may not have enough time to juggle work, family, and college coursework. They worry that their work and family obligations won't leave them time to succeed in college, and they are accustomed to being successful. They worry about how they might fit in with what they think will be much younger classmates. They worry because it has been a long time since they were engaged in academic work, and that their academic skills have dulled over time.

These are difficult obstacles indeed. However, these students bring certain strengths of character that in concert with a supportive Tift College environment enables the vast majority to overcome those obstacles. They are resilient. They already have a history of overcoming obstacles in their lives. They are focused. They aren't in college because their parents want them to be. They are here because they want to be, and they have committed their own resources to the task. They are highly motivated. Unlike younger, traditional students who may be simply exploring possibilities, our students know exactly what they want to achieve. They want to become teachers!

Our students bring experience and maturity to the Tift College program, and they find that the program is well suited to who they are and what they want to achieve. They begin the program gently, a little unsure about their academic skills and abilities. They soon learn that it is hard. And they also learn that it is doable. They become part of a cohort that will proceed through the program almost as a unit. This cohort quickly becomes a tight knit group that provides emotional and academic support for each member. Members watch out for each other in many ways, and they take nearly as much pride in each other's progress as in their own. Before long, they all become active, confident, and successful participants in the program.

It is a joy to teach this richly experienced, mature group of students in the Regional Academic Centers. Because they are focused, I must also be. They want to learn everything they need to know in order to become successful classroom teachers. But they are not interested in extraneous information or information they have already. So each week, for each class, I am challenged to develop lesson plans that respect this experience and maturity, but also bring fresh and useful knowledge to this group.

It's also a joy for me to be able to help these students begin anew because I, too, was once a non-traditional student. Like many of these students, my parents did not graduate from high school, and they were not enthusiastic about any of their children attending college. I recall my mother once saying that universities were full of communists. I also made some unwise and unfortunate decisions in my late teens that kept me from attending college full time after high school. Thankfully, there was what was then referred to as the extension division of the local university. We just called it "night school." After a few years of moving auto parts around a warehouse, I realized an urgent need to complete my college education. By enrolling in night school, I was able to keep my job, pay the rent, and collect some college credits. I had completed some coursework in the "real" university, but the classes were large and I never felt connected. But the extension classes were wonderful. They were small, so we all had to participate, and we all felt like a part of the class. The instructors I had were superior, and we all got to know each other. There were no anonymous lectures in these classes. I recall that it was a history teacher there who rekindled my interest in learning and in continuing in pursuit of a degree. And to top it off, there was free parking.

So I am personally indebted to non-traditional education, and I feel as though my teaching in the Regional Academic Centers has brought my academic life full circle. My hope is that some of our graduates will look back one day and remember me as one of the teachers who made a difference their lives. They certainly make a difference in mine.

Can You Teach a Rock?

Karen Michael, Ph.D.

My aim as an educator is to model the enjoyment of my craft by demonstrating effective teaching strategies, a love of knowledge, and a love of people. I desire to immerse my students in ways that they can be great teachers. I try to demonstrate that effective practices of teaching and learning are rarely based on completing worksheets, listening passively to a dull lecture, or working independently in silence. I want them to observe a variety of instructional strategies to use with their future students. I want my students to know the purpose of every objective, every assessment, and every activity. I want them to realize the value of acquiring the new information, to own it, and make it theirs. These are my goals as I continue to strive to be the best teacher that I can be.

I love being a teacher! It is in my blood. If I am not teaching, I am not complete. I slowly begin to fade near the end of July because I typically do not teach in the summer. I feel myself begin to wither. Quickly, I start planning for the upcoming year in anticipation of new students. It recharges my passion for teaching. I also seek therapy by visiting the school supply aisles at Wal-Mart. I breathe in the intoxicating smell of new school supplies. I gaze at the colorful folders, buy a new pack of pens, and listen to the excitement of children and parents as they load up their carts. The beginning of the academic year is magical. It is a fresh start. It is the thrill of learning new things and meeting new people. The choices of backpacks, lunch boxes, and notebooks are exhilarating. To me, starting school is more significant than New Year's Day. It is a time to set high expectations. Children and teachers get an opportunity to refine their thoughts, behaviors, and hopes.

I started teaching when I was four years old. I had an imaginary class complete with my own chalkboard and pointer. Bobby, my cat, was the only live student at the time. The other students were dolls and stuffed animals. I would get frustrated if a stuffed animal fell over and went to "sleep." Even at a very young age, I began to modify my instruction to engage every learner, even the droopy stuffed elephant who had a habit of sleeping while in my school. Later, I was able to add my sister, Leigh, as a student and any neighborhood child who happened to walk by the open garage door. Little did they know that big wheel races would have to be put on hold until we conquered the alphabet song.

I've always known that I would be a teacher. Pedagogy can be taught to an extent, but there are some people that just possess a natural ability to teach and engage others in their quest for knowledge. I have the gift. I also have the knowledge thanks to an excellent education. Teaching is both an art and a science. An effective teacher must have both to be truly amazing.

The keys to effective teaching and learning in the classroom are exhibiting enthusiasm, possessing a caring attitude, always seeking knowledge, thinking quickly, being organized, being thoughtful, having your materials ready, being prepared through thorough planning, and never forgetting a little magical fairy dust. The goal is to maintain the students' interest and motivation as they acquire new information. Encouraging students to strive for excellence is my main objective as a teacher. I want my students to be thinkers and to enjoy their work. I want it to be impossible for students to have a sour attitude in my classroom. I want to radiate a caring disposition and a passion for teaching.

I attempt to treat my students like my own children. I mean to suggest that I care for them and nurture their needs academically and often personally. I am their advocate. I want them to be successful and to take responsibility for their success. As a teacher, it is my responsibility to educate, guide, and correct my students when they are in my charge, just like a mother. I try to instill this idea when teaching pre-service teachers. I encourage my pre-service teachers to treat their future students the way they would want a teacher to treat their own children.

My passionate beliefs about teaching grew out of my experiences as a child in school, a teacher of children from infants through the eighth grade, a teacher of pre-service teachers, and as a mom. These experiences have culminated together to establish my joyful passion for teaching and learning. The best part is that it is never-ending. I am a lifelong learner and teacher working diligently to enhance my abilities through the scholarship of teaching. While doing this, I am also enhancing the learning of my students' abilities.

For example, I really enjoy teaching at the university level. Tonight I have class and I am so excited! My class tonight is eager to learn, and I am eager to teach them.

Teaching is like a Broadway show. I feel that if my university classes are not worth $200.00 a night (average tuition cost), then I failed. When students attend my class, I want it to be worth the effort. I do not want my students to think about their grocery lists, car problems, or the bills they need to pay. I want their full attention.

I try my best to put on a great show. I even check my dress and my make-up in my dressing room (office) before I walk on stage (in the classroom). Shortly before class, I make final notes, double check my lines (lesson plans), review my Power Point presentation, and walk out with the first of usually three loads of resources for my students. When I share my resources, it is similar to "Show and Tell." As a teacher-education professor, I want to share my children's books, textbooks, lesson plan ideas, resources, great handouts, and samples of children's work.

I announce to the other professors on the office hall, "It's show time. Have a great class." You can feel the energy in the office hall; hear the shuffling of papers as the professors organize themselves for class. There's excitement in the air as 5:30 approaches. It's time! Class has started. My lipstick looks great. I have planned well and I am ready. Four hours later, I have given an excellent performance. Sometimes, my students even clap. Sometimes, I have to let class out early and my students are disappointed. When your students want more, you know you've done an excellent job. After class, I am mentally and physically exhausted, but yet I am still excited. I'm wired because the evening was a success. When I get home, I can't get to sleep. My adrenaline is still up. I take notes as I reflect on the evening. I think about what worked, what did not work, if I left any gaps, and if the students' responses were accurate. I keep these notes and discuss them with my students the following week. This is one example of how I consistently try to point out effective strategies and model them for my pre-service teachers so they can witness my successes and my failures as a teacher.

I used to treasure a child's statement that said, "When I grow up, I want to be just like you." Now what I treasure, as a literacy and language education professor, is when one of my pre-service teachers makes a similar statement. I am thankful and in awe.

I am delighted that I have offered some curriculum and instruction practices that will be useful as that teacher enters the field of teaching armed with an assortment of strategies. I am so glad that I am in the profession of teaching because I feel that I am making a difference.

When I taught fifth grade, I had a student named Brent. He was diagnosed with an emotional behavior disorder. He was living with a wonderful foster family because his mother was a cocaine addict. Brent had some weaknesses in reading. We worked together on his weaknesses. After one particularly difficult lesson, he looked at me in wonder and said, "Mrs. Michael, you are so creative and patient, you could teach a rock." To this day, it is the best compliment that I have ever received. Thanks to Brent, I try to implement creative teaching methods and remember to be patient with the ability levels of all students.

Miss Rogers

Emilie Warner Paille, Ed.D.

Miss Rogers stood by the door to her Algebra II classroom, her arms folded in front of her. She neither smiled nor spoke. In most parts of the school, the bell that signaled the changing of classes created explosions of students out of classrooms, but not in Miss Roger's hall. We walked quieter there than anywhere; couples did not stand close together behind the open classroom doors; and locker stops were quick and efficient. I felt sorry for my friends who were in her classes. Her demeanor was formidable.

The minute the bell rang for class to begin, Miss Rogers would unfold her arms and put one hand on the doorknob, pulling the door behind her and walking with it until it clicked closing teacher and students inside.

It was different across the hall where my Algebra I class met, where we, too, settled into our seats and talked until Mr. Grant left his desk in the front of the room and wrote the page numbers for that day's assignment on the board. We worked the problems on Blue Horse loose-leaf notebook paper and our unfinished classwork became homework, due the next day. I always had plenty of that for two reasons. First, the class was always interesting because a lot went on in there that had nothing to do with math, and second, I couldn't work the problems alone. Just before the bell rang at the end of every class period, Mr. Grant would remind us to finish the assignment for homework, and we'd stack our books, ready to pour back into the hall.

I'm not sure just when algebra got past me, but it was early that year. For a while, I'd been able to read the textbook and understand what to do to work the problems, but as soon as I was unsure, I was stuck. As the weeks went on, I became less able to complete the assignments. By the end of the first semester, I was relieved to see that my algebra grades were C for the first quarter and D for the second quarter, averaging C for my semester permanent record grade. The C allowed me to continue the extracurricular activities I wanted and kept me from having to repeat the course. Armed with those grades and little knowledge, I began the second semester of Algebra I.

I was as lost at the beginning, but it didn't matter because my good friend, I'll call her Wendy, had a brother and a sister just older than we were, and they both did well in algebra. Each night, Wendy would get help from them for her homework, and she'd call me. Over the phone, she would tell me, step by step, exactly what to do. I'd write the problems as she described them and turn in my paper the following day. This allowed me to maintain a perfect score on my homework grades, but my test grades brought my average down and at the end of the second semester, I again earned C, D, C. I wasn't proud, but I don't remember worrying about it either, until the next fall.

In homeroom, the first day of school, I received my schedule and there was Miss Rogers's name and room number right there in black and white. I had expected to have

Mr. Grant again, for it was common practice at our school to have the same teacher for both years of algebra. I was far less than excited. Now I was one of the students who broke away from the mass in the hall to walk beneath Miss Rogers's watchful eye. My memory of walking into her classroom is that she was much taller than the rest of us, that her folded arms were at my eye level. This couldn't be, of course. But she was bigger than life, and her no-nonsense manner outside the classroom continued inside as she called us by our last names and addressed us as Sister and Brother. I was Sister Warner. It's no surprise that no one in her class goofed off. In fact, it was the rare exception for someone to ask for a hall pass to the restroom or the office or to see another teacher. No one ever asked to return to a locker to retrieve forgotten books or papers.

In class that first day, she explained her rules: be on time, be ready for class to begin when the bell rang, and be sure to do the homework. Class time would be working time, and we shouldn't hesitate to ask questions. Each of us would have the opportunity to work problems on the board several times every week. We could take the math book with us to the board, but no notes. Everyone remaining in their desks would work the problems assigned on paper and would be prepared to check them. After working the assigned problems, we were to stay there and wait; no one was to leave the board until all problems were solved and explained to the class. There wouldn't be a lot of homework, but we could expect to have some each day. She then told us to get paper and pencils out to begin work. The first day of school! To say that I was apprehensive would be a gross under-representation; I was terrified!

The prospect of going to the board to work any algebra problem would have been bad enough, but to have to do so in front of my friends and other classmates was tantamount to disaster. I wouldn't have been enthusiastic about working problems on the board even if I had known how to do so, and I couldn't do algebra without Wendy and her brother and sister. But when I was sent to the board a few days later, it wasn't so horrible at all.

Why wasn't it? I ask myself now, from the distance of many years of being a student and even more years of being a teacher. Why wasn't it pure torture? Why didn't the back of my neck burn as I stood there, chalk in hand, empty board before me, struggling to work a problem I knew nothing about? Why wasn't I frantic with embarrassment and knowledge of impending failure? Yet I know the answer to my own questions. It's this: I understood what to do. I knew how to make sense of the abstract language of algebra because I had been led to understand.

I can still see that classroom with its cement block walls. Windows covered one entire side from the top of the room to about four feet from the floor, and another wall held a bulletin board. The two remaining walls held chalkboards and met in an L-shape in the corner of the room. I can almost hear the chalk sounds of eight or ten students working problems and the clinks on the chalkboard tray as the chalk was dropped after solutions were found. I remember the feeling of success when the problems I worked appeared as if by magic in front of me. There were butterflies in my stomach for each of my turns at the board, but not the lead bats I had expected.

Why not? There had to be more than just walking into that room that allowed me to understand. And although I don't remember it, she must have taught me what to do, in manageable steps, before she sent me to the board because I could solve the problems once I was there. I no longer needed Wendy and her family resources to do more than barely pass algebra.

I can still see Miss Rogers, walking the length of the chalkboards and back, watching the work on the board, stopping to assist where needed. She spoke so that only those addressed could hear her and asked questions of students, sometimes pointing at some part of work in progress. There were plenty of erasers at the board and no threat or criticism in using them. I don't remember ever feeling embarrassed as I stood there at the board because when I hit a bump, she nudged me over it. She supported me, and everyone else, too, in learning algebra.

I knew even then that Miss Rogers was a teacher who taught me in ways I could understand. The written evidence of my knowledge was that, except for the first semester, I made A's in Algebra II, but more important than those A's is the fact that I had learned.

As I look back now and think about this experience from a teaching/learning perspective, I realize that Miss Rogers was a teacher who was willing to go back and meet me, as her student, where I was in mathematics when I came into her class. She didn't start right in with her Algebra II textbook and second-year algebra plans because if she had, I would have failed. I hadn't brought with me any foundation from the first year. If she had been the kind of teacher who taught the subject instead of the student, I would have remained clueless about algebra. She must have been willing to go back, see what her students knew, fill in gaps in learning, and proceed from there. She didn't blame me for what I didn't know, in spite of the fact that I had taken no responsibility for my own learning the previous year. She did the proverbial rolling up of her sleeves as she set the tone, the demands, the expectations for learning. And she taught.

In Miss Rogers's image, I see passion for teaching. It is what we hope to see in the teachers we want for our own children and grandchildren: knowledge, dedication, willingness to know the student, willingness to fill the gaps, and willingness to teach with confidence that yields both knowledge and confidence in the student. It is unwillingness to accept less than the best combined with the willingness to roll up one's sleeves and work. It is not a lofty imparting of knowledge, but it is working hard to insure that learning takes place. It is passion for teaching.

Teaching from the Heart

Mary Kay Bacallao, Ed.D.

I knew I wanted to be a teacher. So I hurried through college, knowing that when I was finished, my dream job was just waiting for me. After spending all those years in school, I was finally going to have a chance to do it my way. In the spring and summer of 1988, I began my job search. As the start of school approached, I panicked. I could not find a job. It really didn't matter to me where I taught, but I knew that I wanted to teach fifth grade. During an interview, the principal of the school asked me just one question, "Have you ever taught minority students before?"

I assured him that I had taught minority students and that I could do the job. There were several minority students at the private school where I had just completed my student-teaching assignment. I was offered the job teaching fifth grade at North County Elementary School in Dade County, Miami, Florida. I was elated. I had just two teacher workdays before school was to start. I spent the remainder of that day filling out paperwork.

The next morning, I reported to work. "Where is my classroom?" I asked. They took me down to Pod 22. It was a huge open space. Two other teachers had already set up their classrooms in other sections of Pod 22. I noticed that there were no walls between the sections. There was a pile of junk in my assigned section. Then I was overtaken by the smell that was coming from the boy's restroom next to my assigned area.

Questions filled my mind. Where are the books? Where are the desks and chairs? Where am I going to put up my bulletin boards? My immediate list covered the essentials—classroom furniture and curriculum materials. I must admit that classroom furniture was my first priority. I picked through the pile of broken desks and chairs to find some that might be usable. Most of them did not have all four screws in the seat and wobbled, but I arranged them anyway. I was unable to locate a teacher's desk, so I used a rectangular table. I got rid of any extra junk by putting it outside. We had about half of a class-set of math textbooks. There were several different reading series books. I called for the custodian to clean the boy's bathroom. I checked out an overhead projector from the media center; that was my mainstay for some time.

When I give advice to teacher-education students on how to approach setting up a classroom for the first time, I always tell them that they should focus on the curriculum first. They should do their lesson plans and then set up their room based on the curriculum needs and what they plan to do. But that is not what I did. I gave all my immediate attention to the arrangement of the classroom and left the lesson planning to do over the weekend.

The other teachers watched as I hurried around, trying to get my classroom together. Then, the grade chair called a meeting. I was so excited about our first grade-level meeting. I was one of three fifth-grade teachers. It wasn't too hard to meet because we were in a huge open room together all the time anyway. As instructed, we brought our assigned class lists to the meeting. In order to better meet the needs of the individual students, we decided to group the students for reading and language arts. During a two-hour block of time, the students would be with another teacher. Each student had a placement card with achievement and behavior information. We put all our cards together. The grade chair rearranged the cards into new piles. It was decided that I would teach the lowest group. As I looked through the cards, it was clear that I was dealt what some teachers may call an "unfortunate hand." I commented that my group only had one girl. Many of them also had poor behavior ratings. "You are so young and have so much enthusiasm," said the grade chair. "You can do it."

"No problem," I said.

I woke up bright and early with a spring in my step as I approached my first day with the students. I had everything ready. Assorted books were piled on the desks with nameplates and lesson plans. As the students came in one by one, I greeted them and smiled.

The students settled into their assigned seats and a parent, one of the two parents I saw that day, came up to greet me. "You look nervous," she said.

I didn't feel nervous. I was happy and excited to meet my students. When she said that, I looked around me and realized that I was the only person in the entire pod that was not black, with the exception of Omar, who did not speak English. It did not bother me.

"No," I said. "I'm not nervous."

"Is this your first year as a teacher?"

"Yes, it is," I said.

"I'll pray for you," she said.

"Thank you so much," I responded as I shook her hand.

The bell rang and school began. I went over the class rules and I could tell that they really didn't know what to make of me at first, but I was smiling and they were smiling right back at me. There were times when I could not understand what they were trying to say. For example, when I took attendance, the students responded, "He ain't here. He at the sto." I wondered what the sto was. Several of the students tried to explain, but they kept using the same word. Eventually, it dawned on me, 'Oh, you mean he is at the store!"

Homeroom went well, and then it was time to switch classes for reading and language arts. As the new group of students came, I noticed that many of them were taller than I had expected. The only girl in the class just looked at all the boys around her and put her head down on the desk with a moan. I tried to learn names, but one of the students would not tell me what his name was. Some of the other students called him Froggie. As I tried to get him to tell me his name, he told me that he was going to get his brother and come back after school and shoot me dead. For some reason, it seemed as if the whole pod stopped to hear how I would respond.

There was a long pause and the pod was silent for a moment as I thought about what to say.

"Is that so?" I said. "Could you please repeat what you just said? I would like to get the whole thing down so I can tell your mother about it."

"Augh, no, I was just playing with you. I didn't mean it," said Froggie.

"Is that so?" I said.

At that moment, I decided that I would have to show them that I meant business, but I would still be nice. In those first few weeks, on more than one occasion, I prayed to ask God for wisdom in how to teach.

When the school bell rang at the end of that first day, I waved goodbye to the students as they ran out of the class. Then the custodian came in and took a look around.

"Must be your first year," he said. "You know, you should get the students to clean up before you let them go home."

"I think that is a great idea," I said. I had never really thought about dismissal procedures, but I was on my way to becoming a transforming practitioner.

I was tired at the end of every day, but very happy. When I got my first paycheck, I looked at it and thought, "Wow! I am getting paid for doing this!" It was amazing that I could do something that I really wanted to do and get paid for it too.

As the days went by, I slowly came to the realization that teaching was much different from being in school. Being in charge was a greater responsibility. In those first few weeks of teaching, I knew that something about me had to change if I was going to make a difference with those students. But there were some things about me that I did not want to change. I wanted to be a nice teacher that cared deeply about the success of her students. I never wanted to insult or put my students down. I wanted to treat them with respect always. I would pray for them.

As I observed, firsthand, some of the behavior management techniques of the teachers I worked with, I was amazed. I wondered in awe how they could have such excellent classroom management. I was wearing myself out with both "positive reinforcement" and "consequences for misbehavior," trying to get my students to pay attention and do their work. But it seemed as if it was effortless for them. Their students just did exactly what they said. One of the other fifth-grade teachers in particular had amazing control over her students. Her line was always perfectly straight. Then one day, a few weeks into the school year, I saw her jabbing a pencil into the arm of one of the students that had stepped slightly out of line. In class, when one of the students challenged her, she said, "Now if you think you are going to act like that then you, me, and that table are going to be on the floor because I don't play."

A few days later, we had a parent come into the pod unannounced. She walked right through my class into another teacher's area. "Don't you be messing with my son," she said, "I'll be back with my gun and I'll be sending you to the morgue."

Then she stormed out. We all decided to buzz the office and lock the doors as the panic spread throughout the pod. They must have been busy that day in the office because they did not respond. So we spent the next few hours with all the doors locked. Then, someone knocked on the door. It was by my area, so I went over to open it.

"No, Miss Fanning, don't open the door!" Some of my students yelled.

Most of my class took cover under their desks. But when I slowly opened the door, just a crack, I was relieved to see that it was only one of the paraprofessionals.

Those times brought us together as a class. We enjoyed being together. We worked, laughed, and played together. Recess was just outside the pod. It was a wonderful thing to see the students playing when you know that you have been working hard all morning. The girls jumped rope and the boys played football. Sometimes I would toss the ball around with them too. I couldn't say there was a student in my class that I didn't like.

That was the year that Officer Lozano had shot and killed a black man fleeing on a motorcycle in Miami, Florida. Racial tensions were high in the city. We talked about it in class. I listened to what they had to say. We talked about what choices they would have made. I think I began to understand them, and I think they understood that I was a white woman who cared about them. One of the students, Shatril, had invited me to visit her church, and I was honored to attend with my fiancé, Aldo Bacallao.

On the last day of school, I brought some flowers for the girls and most of us cried as we said goodbye. I don't remember if I brought anything for the boys. We had made T-shirts that read, "I Survived Pod 22!" We would miss Pod 22 and all the memories of that year. Years later, I was hosting a videoconference at St. Thomas University with the Miami Museum of Science. One of my students from that year, Shatril, recognized me. We made arrangements to get together. She was a now a graduate of the University of Miami, a biology major. It was her mother who had said she would pray for me on that first day We reminisced about that year and she filled me in on how some of the other students in the class were doing. I told her about all the mistakes I had made that year as I laughed and she told me she hadn't noticed any of them. We talked about our faith and how we had both changed over the years, but somehow we had stayed the same.

In looking back on almost nine years of elementary school teaching and now seven years of university teaching, I do laugh at my first experiences. I have learned not to let people or circumstances that may appear challenging to change me into someone I do not want to be. Using intimidation may have excellent short-term results, but that method eventually backfires. Mutual respect, consistency, and real concern for students are more effective over the years.

One of the misconceived notions that I had when I began was that all my students would be like me when I was in school: conscientious, hardworking, and well-behaved. When I realized that not every student was like me, I had to adjust my approach. Not all students arrived in school with a burning desire to learn. I had to get their attention and instill in them the joy of learning. I had to make learning meaningful to them. I also had to come to the realization that even if you treat people well, they will not always treat you the same way, but even that is still OK. One of my teacher-education students was thinking aloud one day and said something like this, "Well, I thought that if I was nice to them and gave them candy, they would be nice to me too."

Not true. Being nice to your students will not always get them to behave. I am not saying that being mean works either; it doesn't. Please don't think you have to give them candy. Their parents may not appreciate it, and their dentist will definitely not appreciate it. Your job is to teach them, not sugar them up. You have to require your students to behave; do not accept anything less. It is not about how nice you are. It is not about how mean you are. They will misbehave if you let them. So don't let them.

In working with disadvantaged students, don't let your sympathy for their situation deter you from teaching them to reach their fullest potential. In my first few years, I was overcome with pity for them and I am not sure that I challenged them as I now know I could have. The same is true with college students. Many of them have full-time jobs and families to take care of. But we don't do them any favors by not requiring them to do their very best because if we do, they might not be fully prepared to enter any classroom and succeed when they graduate.

After my first month of teaching, the teachers in the pod commented that they were both wondering when I would talk myself out. Maybe they thought that I talked too much. But, after all, they did have to listen to me all day, every day. I don't really remember hearing them say very much. When both of them had specials, and the music and Spanish teachers came in, the two classes would have paper airplane wars, and eventually, I gave up and decided to take my class outside when the other teachers were on break. But most of the time, the other two sections would be quietly working and I would talk about whatever subject matter we were doing and interact with my students. In looking back on my original method of "teacher talk" or what might now be called "direct instruction with interaction," or maybe even "the Socratic method," I realize that I may have overdone it. If teaching is talking and learning is listening, then one could say that I did my job and the students did theirs. But I do believe that teaching has to be more than talking and learning is what happens individually as each student processes information. As in most things, there is a balance to be reached. Teachers do have to talk to initiate thinking and problem-solving. But getting the students to read, write, think, and interact with the curriculum materials, other students, and the teacher is more important than I first realized.

One of the things that I have enjoyed about being a teacher is that inside your classroom, you can make things happen. If you have a great idea or interesting way of teaching something, you can accomplish it. You can work with the students to decorate your classroom and make it a great place to be. You can set the tone for learning. If you want everyone to get along, you just let your students know that you expect them to get along. It is your own little world, and you try to make it a great place to be so that the students learn and grow. In all the coursework I have taken in educational leadership, I have heard about how important the principal is. Now, I know that the principal is important, but I think the teachers are more important. Why? Because the teacher is the one who is in the classroom everyday, making things happen for the students. A great principal cannot exist without great teachers. But a great teacher can exist without a great principal.

I have often thought about those bean sprouts that students grow in the spring. Students are like those sprouts. As much as we want to help them learn, grow, and mature, we cannot force those leaves out of the seeds. All we can do is provide them with the soil, the water, and the sunshine.

Those seeds will grown and sprout when they are ready. Sometimes it is a matter of waiting to see that the methods we are using are working. Learning cannot be forced just as those leaves cannot be forced out of the seeds that contain them. As much as I say that it is up to us, the teachers, it is really not up to us alone. It is a combination of home, school, and community that work together to nurture our young children. We do not work alone, but in a larger community of support for our students.

Being a teacher is not like any other profession. It carries with it a greater responsibility. Parents, unbelievably, have entrusted us with their greatest gift, their children. It is our job to be worthy of that trust. It is not a job to be taken lightly. So with this in mind, let us do our best to learn how to be effective teachers.

Building Joyful, Passionate Relationships

Janet Smith Fields, Ed.D.

As I come to reflect upon my own joyful passion for teaching, I am struck by the nature of those two words—joyful and passion—and how they have been exhibited throughout my teaching career. Joy, children—learners of all ages—bring joy to my life. One of my earliest experiences was in the lab school at Georgia Southern University. One bright, young, out-of-bounds four-year-old insisted on calling everyone "dum-dum." As we had been properly instructed in the appropriate manner of managing, correcting young children, my response to her was, "My name is Ms. Fields; I would like for you to call me Ms. Fields," to which she promptly replied, "Hello, Dum-Dum Ms. Fields!"

Joy, yes, teaching is joyful. Another remembrance brings forth that first year in a second-grade classroom with my young "Dennis the Menace." Dennis, as I will call him, challenged me from day one with his many antics, sharpening crayons in the pencil sharpener, tossing his shoes on top of the building to which he explained, "I was just shaking the dirt out." And then there were the poor hamsters Flip and Geraldine. One day I left several girls with Dennis in the room during recess to clean the hamster cages while I took a quick restroom break. Upon reentering the classroom, I found the girls hysterical and poor Geraldine flat on her back in the cage with her legs straight up in the air and Dennis standing to the side very subdued. When I asked what had happened, the girls quickly explained that Dennis had placed Geraldine into an empty toilet paper tube, closed both ends with his hands, and shook the tube rapidly back and forth several times. We were all certain that the poor hamster had met her demise. As I began to scold Dennis, Geraldine suddenly began to stir and come back to life. We had a difficult, if not impossible, task from that day forward keeping Geraldine in the cage. Most every night she would escape and engage in various escapades throughout the school, once ending up in the vault in the principal's office!

Joy comes in many forms and is certainly not limited to the elementary school. My college-aged students have also brought me tremendous joy. Not so much in their antics in the classroom but in their own life experiences. Loris Malaguzzia, the founding director of the world renowned preschools in Reggio Emilia, was credited as saying that education is about building relationships. Relationships between individuals, between humans and the environment, etc. And so it is in the university classroom when one is preparing teachers. I have used several activities in an effort to develop positive group dynamics in and among students in their undergraduate program. One activity asks the students to develop a representation of themselves that displays on the outside what they are like on the outside, what one sees immediately about them, what they are most willing to share with others, and what is important to them that others are aware of. Then on the inside of this representation, they are to display or present what is on their inside, what are the thoughts, feelings, ideas, emotions, that are not so readily apparent to others. This is a powerful activity, one not used at the very beginning of the group development process, but rather several weeks into the semester. I have been in sessions where students revealed very personal information, many students were crying during the session, and the bonds that developed as a result of this activity held the group together during later times that were trying and potentially contentious. Once I remember a young, unmarried student telling the class, "You may decide that you don't want to have anything to do with me after I tell you that I have a biracial child." The class responded with several students moving over to Sheila, embracing her, and assuring her that they cared for her and would always care for her and would willingly, graciously, and honestly accept her and her child. This activity always takes students down the path of examining their own prejudices and biases and prepares them for the task of developing a nurturing, diverse classroom environment.

The other activity involves students keeping a daily journal reflecting on the ideas presented in class and how these ideas, as well as field experiences, text assignments, outside readings, etc. were influencing their own theories of teaching and learning. Many students have, through the years, expressed to me how during the writing process they actually formed their own theories or in fact changed their ideas about a topic as they were engaged in writing about that topic.

Yes, joy comes from the relationships one builds with students. From laughing with them as they experience life's great moments of engagements, marriages, births, graduations, National Board Certifications, Teacher of the Year awards, etc. And passion comes too, but not always in the same way. For me the passion comes from my soul; from my sense of commitment to my fellow human beings; from the sorrow at loss, at inequity, at the powerlessness of being unable to right the wrongs that so many individuals face.

Passion came early for me in my career with a young kindergartener name Roy Lee. Roy Lee walked to school. In fact, Roy Lee only came to school when he got himself up and dressed and made his own way down the street to the school and into my classroom. It might be 8:00 am or it might be 11:00 am, just whenever he could make it. And when he came he was always hungry, dirty, and smelly from sleeping in the bed with younger brothers and sisters who wet the bed. And when he came, we always made sure that he got something to eat and that he had a safe, loving, caring shelter from the storms of his life. We did what we could for Roy Lee, although I always knew it was never enough. One day, twenty years later, I opened the local paper to read the headlines about a murder that had occurred in our community. A young woman was found stabbed to death, and a young man, accused of the murder, had been arrested, and his picture was there on the front page. As I looked at that picture, the face was familiar, and when I read further I saw the name of the accused murderer, Roy Lee. My heart sank. The passion in my soul raged to the surface, this child never had a chance, as early as five years of age his life had taken a path that led to this very act. After gaining permission from the sheriff, I paid a visit to the jail, taking a few items with me, not knowing what I would say when I saw him but knowing that I could not live without at least trying to contact him. I visited with Roy Lee that day, he did not remember me, his long-ago kindergarten teacher, but I told him that I remembered him, and remembered how he always wanted to learn and how he had come to school to learn and that throughout the years I had remembered him and thought of him often. I offered to be of help to him in any way that I could. He asked that I speak on his behalf during the trial and I assured him that I would. I called his attorney and told her of my former relationship with this young man and that I would be willing to help. She thanked me and told me that she would contact me, I never heard back from her.

Passion for those less fortunate flows from a deep place in your soul and courses through your body and leaves you convicted that you must take a stand for these human beings. I was an assistant principal in an elementary school, and we were working with three children from the same family trying to assess their learning and secure special services for them when their mother moved them to another school in a nearby district. Such a pattern she had followed several times before, moving the children just as they were beginning to settle down and services were about to be offered. This young child, seven years of age, we will call Sonya, came into my office and demanded her balloons. After several minutes of trying to understand what she was saying and why she thought I might have balloons for her, I realized that as other children in the school were sent balloons on their birthdays from their families, this child knew she would not be attending this school on her birthday. Thinking that the office was the responsible party for the balloons, she wanted to secure her prize before moving on. Looking back on this later, I regretted not ordering balloons for this child myself, just so she might have one experience receiving a prize like balloons at school. Several years later I was working at the university supervising student teachers and ran into this same child in another school. I engaged the teacher in a conversation about the welfare of the child and shared my particular interest in her situation. The teacher shared the following poignant story with me about the day the child was very ill with a temperature over 102. The teacher told Sonya that she was going to have to call her mother to come to the school to get her. Sonya pleaded, "Please don't call my mother, let me stay here at school, I won't bother you." My heart broke for this child; the passion flowed through my body. The first thing most children want, when sick with a temperature, is their mother. What must this child's life be like if she is begging to stay at school under these circumstances?

And so, the passion rises and finds a way to express itself in me as I work to prepare future teachers to work with students like Dennis, Roy Lee, and Sonya. And I know that, as said in *Praying for Sheetrock*, "It all begins with one or two people, moving in unison, to share the joy and the passion for teaching with one another, and with future teachers, in an effort to ensure that every child has an equal opportunity to grow and learn."

The Heroes of Modern-Day Education

Peter Ross, Ph.D.

I've marveled at education's union of artful delivery of instruction and appreciation of science that substantiates the practice. Yet despite all that is known, teaching is reported to be immensely challenging. To illustrate the challenges, let's consider the following: every day the teacher stands in front of an audience of students with no script and no true rehearsal. So, what is the curtain call, the rush of exhilaration that keeps those marvelous entrepreneurs of learning committed to the profession?

This story actually begins after hundreds of interviews have taken place. These were not ordinary interviews; they were interviews of hundreds of school-age students ranging in age from five to nineteen years. The interviews were structured so that several questions were common to all students. In particular, responses to two questions have intrigued me over the years.

The first question directed toward students was: "During all of your years in school, who has been your very favorite teacher?" The responses to this question have been remarkably uniform in content. Students required very little deliberation in most cases. It was as if a powerful image of the teacher was etched in their minds. Often, broad smiles emerged as students collected their thoughts to reply. The following is representative of typical responses to this question: "My favorite teacher was strict but fair, hardly ever yelled, and made me feel good [important] about being in her/his class."

What is particularly interesting about these poignant illustrations is that the students were describing the effects of each teacher's behavior-management style. It appears that the teachers who were viewed by students as "most favorite" were likely strong disciplinarians. And, the discipline style appears to be based primarily on positive reinforcement, with limited use of harsh punishers, such as yelling. The students' responses also indicate that positive regard toward humans is universally accepted and cherished.

These revelations are heuristic. Research has shown us that the most effective teachers are those who systematically employ a behavior-management style that emphasizes positive reinforcement and limits use of punishers. Research shows further that humans respond best to these management practices in terms of compliance and motivation toward academics.

A second question was then asked during the student interview. We asked: "Which teacher was your least favorite and why?" Again, responses from students of all ages were very similar in content. The most common response went something like: "My least favorite teacher yelled a lot and was mean. I didn't like being in that classroom."

Although children were articulating adult behavior in their own words, they were saying something profound about teachers. It seems that those being interviewed were conveying strong resignation, disdain, and contempt for adults with weak management skills. Even the youngest children ostensibly recognized weak teachers when they utilized frequent punitive measures for discipline. There was a personal vulnerability expressed by these young people, that being in a poorly managed classroom was psychologically frightening. On an unconscious level for many, students recognized that ineffective discipline is imbued with harshness, negativity, or criticism.

Is all of this a profound tale or a prescription for duty as a professional educator? Likely it is both. As a teacher and the reader of this passage, it is incumbent upon you to make choices for impacting young people's lives. Will you choose to be the "yeller?" Or will you make strides toward carving out powerful and fond memories for young humans under your aegis? Really, the choice is clear.

The "curtain call" comes when teachers successfully integrate respect for young people, master the content, and demonstrate sound behavior management skills. Then, the profession is not regarded as drudgery, or at best, as challenging, but as rewarding. What a wonderful place to be in one's profession! Isn't this an educator's formula for fulfillment, ego strength, and well-being?

Equipping Students with Digital Media to Communicate Their Understanding

M. Randall Spaid, Ph.D.

I marveled as I watched Mandy connecting her laptop computer to the LCD projector and a portable sound system. She smiled proudly as she launched her QuickTime digital story and previewed it before class. Mandy had spent many hours creating her reflection on her fieldwork in a local high school English class. As she shared her movie, her classmates and I were captivated as she used the metaphor of making lemonade from lemons to describe the challenges she faced of working with a class of low-achieving ninth-graders.

This was a class assignment, and in order to create this movie and share her experience in a multimedia format, Mandy used intuitive iMovie™ software on a powerful Macintosh computer to merge digital images of her students with a script she recorded and a musical soundtrack that complemented her narrative. The diverse images, transitions, special effects, and music kept us engaged in her story.

To put together the elements that made up her movie, Mandy determined what she wanted to say, she selected the pictures, she wrote the script, and she chose music that would complement the pictures and enhance her story. Her passion become apparent as she explained why she chose to be a classroom teacher, a unique story told in a unique way. As her classmates and I listened to her story, we were almost transported into Mandy's classroom; her descriptions evoked strong feelings about who these kids are and how teachers can make a difference in their lives. She described a challenging situation and used the analogy of being handed lemons and making lemonade through sheer determination. Her use of technology enabled us to meet her students; when I looked at her images I remembered my own experiences with students like this. Mandy's story would not have had the same impact on us if she had "debriefed" us without an interactive movie.

As teachers in the classroom, we have the opportunity to be innovative and creative. Since we know our students, we can select diverse multimedia resources and infuse digital media in our lessons that captivate their interest and, hopefully, teach more effectively. I learned how to engage my students successfully during many years of teaching high school science. As I modified the traditional or "typical" classroom environment, my students slowly transformed into more intentional, independent learners.

My biology students were eager to begin dissection of a frog during the amphibians unit; however, I first taught them how to use a laserdisc bar code reader to access an extensive collection of digital photographs of a grass frog's anatomy. They were intrigued by the vivid detail of the internal organs and eagerly explored the vast database with lots of "oohs" and "ahhs." Excitement coursed through the room when they discovered a movie showing a frog's beating heart and another clip showing frogs laying eggs during mating.

We then headed to the computer lab to perform a "virtual" frog dissection. My tech-savvy students were eager to try out their skill using the interactive software's simulated forceps, scissors, and scalpel. There were squeals of delight and success when they made the correct incisions and the virtual frog's skin flaps retracted on screen. Several students spontaneously moved from computer to computer to look over the shoulder of a classmate to offer suggestions and hints. Captivated by the digital dissection instruments and animations, most of them repeated the virtual dissection two or three times; they seemed enthusiastic to learn about frog anatomy and physiology using resources other than a textbook. I later found out that a number of their friends in other biology classes were jealous that our class was in the computer lab while their learning was limited to pictures and passages in a biology textbook.

After they completed the dissection simulation in the computer lab, my students returned to my biology lab to explore a preserved grass frog. Since the laserdisc of frog anatomy images was still setup, they did not hesitate to access the photo gallery as a reference. I listened to their animated chatter with delight as they compared the laserdisc pictures and virtual dissection images with the actual specimens in their dissection pans. Although it was a lot of work to setup the electronic technologies and train my students to use them, I was rewarded by their sustained engagement and high achievement. After each class, my students told me that this lesson was "awesome" or "really cool," and I am convinced that my teaching strategies using digital media were worth the effort.

During a botany unit infused with electronic technology, I provided my students with marigold seeds, potting soil, plastic pots, and a digital camera. Each team of students took photographs at the beginning of each class as their seeds germinated and the seedlings grew. They excitedly compared their pictures to their classmates' pictures as flower buds appeared and the flowers opened. Downloading the images to a computer to generate a time-lapse sequence captured their imagination and prompted diverse conversations about plant growth and physiology. I was impressed and immensely proud of their accomplishment when they presented the multimedia slideshow to a raucous chorus of affirmation and praise. Providing the resources and digital tools for this activity was arduous, but the dynamic learning environment made a difference, and I was gratified by their enthusiasm and hard work.

The task of motivating adolescents is sometimes daunting, but a project may engage them if using digital tools is intriguing or provocative. My design-a-critter project assignment for a zoology unit seemed to inspire my biology students to be creative when they discovered that they would use photo-editing and drawing software. In the role as genetic engineers, they were directed to design an organism that could survive on a fictitious planet, "Aquaterra." Their animated chatter and excitement energized me.

To coexist with indigenous life forms and find a niche in one of Aquaterra's diverse habitats, my students used Web and CD-ROM resources to research the adaptations of animals we studied. Then, they used the computer to create their own creatures with unique characteristics and names, such as the "Barkish," a furry and fishlike critter engineered to live in Aquaterra's polar sea; the "Mandix," a peculiar venomous, flying marsupial adapted to inhabit the Temperate forest; and the apelike "Mapu," a quasi-terrestrial predator designed to live in the Rocky Crags of Aquaterra. The computer lab buzzed with excitement as my students generated their virtual critter and debated the logic of the features they selected for a specific habitat. Students with more experience using the software readily assisted classmates who were eager to create surreal images.

I was mesmerized at my students' sophisticated presentations when they shared the results of their genetic engineering project in a simulated scientific symposium. They quickly mastered the digital tools and stayed on task for long periods of time in and outside of class in order to share their understanding of phylogenetics in a unique way. They reveled when their peers exclaimed, "That's awesome!" and "Wow, that is *way* cool!" I, too, applauded their accom-plishments, elated that the digital media I enticed them for the design-a-critter project with were useful tools for learning.

Unfortunately, these powerful technology tools and digital media available to enhance teaching and learning often gather dust in a media center storage room because teachers are not trained to use them or do not adopt them as an instructional strategy. I believe in an eclectic approach to the design of instruction. Technology can best be integrated into instruction when viewed from the perspective of the teacher, not of the technologist, so I approach digital media and technology resources in terms of the day-to-day challenges of teachers, with real everyday teaching issues, in real content areas, involving real media and materials.

In my classroom, I turned to digital media to strengthen my students' basic skills. Video and audio clips brought class material to life in a way that stimulated my young science students' minds and facilitated learning. By incorporating pictures, sounds, and animations for pond succession during an ecology unit, my students took virtual fieldtrips to explore the interactions between plants and animals in a different way. Paper-and-pencil projects gave way to dynamic slideshows and web pages in my effort to lure them into science curiosity and conversation.

My fervent belief that technology can enhance instructional activities compelled me to assess my students' learning and instructional needs. Teachers have a responsibility to identify best practices for integrating technology into instruction appropriate to every discipline. Teaching is like the *Mission: Impossible* series. In every episode of *Mission: Impossible*, Mr. Phelps was handed a directive that would self-destruct five to ten seconds after reading; then, the team would set out to accomplish the challenging task.

Teachers today have been presented with the same kind of daunting, Sisyphean task. Every high school teacher seems to encounter students who whine, "This is stupid," "Why do we need to learn this junk?" and "This is boring!" A teacher's educational philosophy surfaces not in esoteric educational jargon, but in a consistent and determined response to dismantling these verbal barriers and assisting students in their learning.

Often my job seems impossible, I am expected to prepare students for high-stakes testing, compel them to think critically, problem-solve, work cooperatively and collaboratively with their peers, and demonstrate effective communication using advanced technology in their class projects. This shopping list of expectations for teachers is what state legislators and education reformers want. The business community has its own wish list; and parents have disparate expectations of schools, too, since they value education based upon their unique background and socioeconomic status. So how does one survive when standing in the vortex of these whirling demands?

Brain research tells us that people learn when the information has emotional impact (everyone remembers what they were doing at 9:30 AM on 11 September 2001), or when the information seems valuable. Since today's youth value computers and readily integrate technology in their day-to-day lives, digital media tools used by teachers in the classroom add value and have the potential to inspire adolescents to sustain their engagement.

As we acknowledge our students' individual strengths and encourage independent, self-directed learning, we can enhance their deeper learning and critical thinking skills. Just like the *Mission: Impossible* team, teachers must utilize state-of-the-art technological gadgets and tools to engage our students. Many experienced teachers have a tacit understanding of classroom dynamics and can address their multiple intelligences and diverse learning styles of adolescents. An assignment to create a digital story like Mandy did has potential to change the way teachers view project work and facilitate more authentic assessment of what our students are learning. We have the knowledge, the digital tools, the expertise, and the passion to provide authentic learning opportunities—these inspire us to continue as teachers when we experience the thrill of learning with our students.

I Will Teach

Tracy Knight Lackey, Ph.D.

Given my flair for drama, I was quite certain that I would have an Oscar or Tony by now. Obviously the universe had other plans because I am a teacher, and happily so. I am not dismayed at the lack of instant results, rather I move in faith as I may never see the effects of my teaching and efforts come to fruition in my students. I am not disappointed by the mediocre monetary compensation as I have access to the most valuable possessions on earth: minds and hearts. I am not reticent to reach out to everyone important in the holistic development of a child even if I am received in a hostile manner because I emerge from every encounter stronger, with greater integrity, and with patience rivaling that of Job.

To be honest, I concede that there have been times when I seriously considered a career change, but I always came back to my senses and my center. I will not, I shall not be moved in any direction other than delightfully forward. My rationale for doing so cannot be explained in a simple statement or single theory. My passion for teaching emanates from heuristic experiences and encounters with people whom I have respected, loved, failed, and, at times, feared.

I teach because Dr. Brooks told me I was something special and in turn I told Cerri. Like many graduate students from families with limited resources, I attended school full-time and supplemented my financial aid by working full-time as long-term substitute teacher. The local director of special education taught my first course. She stood all of four-foot-nine, yet her aura exuded integrity, power, and fearlessness. She was the most keen and challenging teacher I ever had. At the culmination of the semester, she requested a meeting with me. She said, "I want you to know that I think you are special and you should pursue a Ph.D." I am still not certain whether that was a suggestion or an order. Nevertheless, six months later I was enrolled in a doctoral program, and approximately three years later I graduated with a Ph.D. in Special Education. I began teaching college and one of my first students was Cerri. From the moment class began, she established herself as a dedicated, innovative, intelligent individual who conveyed a level of intellectual maturity rarely evident in novice educators. At the conclusion of the class, I communicated to Cerri what Dr. Brooks had told me years ago. Now it is six years later and as I move on to another institution Cerri is making a similar transition. You see she completed her undergraduate, graduate, and doctoral studies in six years. In the fall she will be an assistant professor of Multicultural Education. She has promised to pass on the simple message that had such a huge impact on both of our lives.

Dr. Brooks taught me, and Cerri confirmed, that words are formidable tools endued with such power as to change an individual who can then change the world.

I teach because of Mia and Do. I went from teaching at an all-black middle school in the South to teaching at a diverse middle school in the Midwest. It was a culture shock to teach at a school where students were black, white, Latino, and Asian. Even thought I felt like a competent teacher, I went through some changes because the children were different. Mia and Do were both my students and one year apart in age. They were from Laos. Mia would come to school tired, inadequately dressed, with dirty hair, while her brother was always rested, neat, and clean. I knew about gender differences in Asian cultures, but I was thinking, "When in Rome do as the Romans do." I lost it when she came to school on a snowy day wearing a T-shirt, shoes with holes in the bottom and without the coat I had gotten for her from a local charity. I asked where her coat was and she said that her mother had given it to her sister. I called and sent notes home but received no word back. Finally, the school social worker, a translator from refugee services, and I made a home visit. In the end I was wrong. The mother was newly immigrated, did not speak English, was very concerned about both of her children, and needed some help getting acclimated to a new world where her cultural practices were easily construed as abuse. What really changed my mind was when she said, "I trust and respect the expertise of teachers and do not want to interfere." It never occurred to me that an act, such as parental involvement, could be viewed as anything other than a right, necessity, and privilege. Mia and Do taught me that teachers must adapt attitudes and behaviors that honor, and thereby include, all families not just our own. Thinking and behaving in solely an autobiographical manner is counterproductive. Honoring diversity does not compromise the right to have personal beliefs and values. Rather it allows us to act in a more appropriate and relevant manner when communicating and working with individuals different than ourselves.

I teach because of Alex. Some days he would come in and be an angel. Other days he would come in and call me every foul name imaginable. I would sometimes get physically ill before school. When Alex was not there, it was a good day. The kids in the school were scared of him and I guess I was too. I documented his behavior, talked to other teachers, called administration downtown, and begged them to come and observe Alex in my class. I didn't know what to do with him. People in the school could see that I was floundering. It was the custodian who told me that Alex's father was in prison for killing his mother, that he lived in a three bedroom apartment in the projects with his grandmother, two young aunts who boosted by selling stolen goods for a living, their six or seven children, and his four siblings. I still didn't know what to do with him after that, but I understood him more. I wish I could say that I made the necessary accommodations and connections that facilitated a wonderful school year. But that did not happen. Alex taught me that teachers/service providers must accept the responsibility for supporting, in some way, every individual critical to the personal and intellectual well-being of a student. Support can mean identifying programs and services that assist families in developing behaviors that will empower them in assuming co-responsibility for their children's learning. Long gone are the days when teaching reading, writing, and arithmetic were sufficient. Enigmas such as high mobility, poverty, and family discord will follow children into our schools and classrooms, therefore we must commit to becoming agents of social change. In some cases teachers are the sole purveyors of stability, a sense of belonging, guidance and even love for children.

I teach because there are Ms. Z's in the world. My mother was a single parent of three who was cognizant of the opportunities, freedoms, and experiences a good education could afford her children. As such, she worked two jobs, while attending nursing school, so that I could attend a private school. I was one of few black students who attended a private Catholic school during my elementary years. Even among the other black students, I was somewhat of a novelty as they all came from two-parent homes. As I think back, one teacher, Ms. Z, still haunts me in some way. She was this very tall, lean, white woman with a cap of salt and pepper hair in a snazzy cut. I remember thinking how beautiful she was and how nice she dressed until she opened her mouth. She ran a very regimented class, but there were special rules for students who were poor, black, and/or those from non-traditional families (I use this term very loosely). For "us" she had a special trick when we did not behave in the way she wanted (this included answering a question wrong, not dressing up to her standards, daring to speak/whisper to a fellow student). She would get in my face, berate me to tears, spit ever so lightly, and pinch me in my armpit. I never told my mother; this was a secret I shared only with the few students who were like me. Once when I was attending graduate school and working at a department store, she came to my counter. Even as an adult I immediately recognized her. Before I could extend a greeting, she was verbally attacking a fellow colleague and me over something that occurred at another counter. This time I was not scared.

Rather I felt pity for this sour and bitter human being and the many children I suspect she has scarred over the years.

Given the need to inspire children to think and move beyond their circumstances, to work for the creation of an equitable and pluralistic society, to view and teach children to thrive in their manifold spaces and roles, and to replace destructive words, influences and mindsets with hope and knowledge I will continue to teach. I will teach until the teachers' lounges becomes a think-tank for generating solutions for serving children and communities instead of a hub of gossip. I will teach until the words retard, dumb, stupid, and impossible are obsolete. I will teach until love, democracy, collaboration, and collective responsibility become essential curricular tools. I will teach until individual differences are deemed opportunities to teach, grow, and learn in exponential ways as opposed to impediments to the "system." I am reasonably certain these changes will not occur in my lifetime; nevertheless I shall depart this earth celebrating the inevitable revolution lead by heroes, lead by teachers.

Because They Had Dreams of the Best Place to Be

Jerry Worley, Ph.D.

They seemed so natural. They had rhythms to their teaching style that affected my own rhythms, my own authenticity as a human being. My favorite teachers reached my needs as a student and as a person. Although, they never provided me with the perfect answer to life's greatest question, these educators seemed to be on a course toward something beyond our five-sensory world; they were leading me toward the final resolution of the Great Mystery. Maybe the answer was somewhere on this earth. Or, maybe it was to be found somewhere beyond the heavens. Or, maybe it was in the very classroom that we found ourselves. These Sages had a method to their teaching style that influenced me to believe that for that moment in time, for that particular class, with those particular students, that this was truly *the best place to be*. For me, it was, "Onward, toward the future." And the future was radiant, sparkling, and shining like the sun emerging over the Rockies.

Ah yes, *the best place to be*.

They Were Authentic

Because of my favorite teachers, teaching is very important to me. Their presence guided us toward our own independence and destiny. As we all know, a good teacher models what they believe in, and accordingly, my favorite teachers appeared to be following the original blueprint of their very existence. They were authentic in the sense that their life's philosophy appeared to match their teaching philosophy. They didn't need any earthly appendages (including other people) to make them whole. One of my favorite teachers was a trust psychologist by the name of Dennis McLoughlin. McLoughlin taught me about The Herd and how the world's favorite teachers would not follow The Herd. They weren't persuaded by The Herd because they had heard that one day The Herd laid palms down for Jesus, and within five days they had crucified him. My favorite teachers appeared to be following the natural rhythms of their blueprint, God's original plan of action; accordingly, they didn't need permission to live.

My favorite teachers understood that teaching was a science-based art form. Yes, there was content, there were foundations, and there were standards to be honored and addressed. But they also understood that by only teaching content they were doing their students a disservice. To them, information was not enough. They understood the importance of more inquiry and less dispensing of potentially worthless and pointless knowledge. Wasn't this more of the same? It was just like Sisyphus's fate: roll the boulder up the hill, to watch it roll back. And this repeated until it becomes a vicious cycle that cannot be broken. Nothing more, but more of the same.

Because my favorite teachers were artists influencing us to reason independently and to be accountable, they naturally guided us to find our own authenticity, our own passions, our own dreams. Thomas Merton once said, "Therefore, whatever you see your soul to desire according to God, do that thing, and you shall keep your heart safe." In my opinion, my favorite teachers' hearts were safe. At the same time, they were also influencing us to find our very own guide to the place where we felt that we ought to be—the best place to be. My heart felt safe in their classrooms because for me, for that moment in time, it was the best place to be.

They Took Responsibility for Their Own Happiness

They dropped it at the door.

Whatever problems, harms, ills, troubles, difficulties, or uncertainties that were potentially hovering around them, they never brought it to class.

Never.

Never, ever.

They knew that problem-centered teachers brought nothing but petty, psychological garbage to the classroom and that it would throw a wrench into the collective resonance of the learning environment.

There's an old saying out West that goes something like this: "It doesn't matter how the jackass got himself into the ditch, the fact is that we have to pull him out." Therefore, we can either throw a fit, or earn the "A." Thank God we have a choice. We can be what McLoughlin called "Doo-Doo Smellers," or we can take full responsibility for our own choices—as well as life's happenstances. We all know that when we were students, we never appreciated teachers who harped on the problem. It affected our classroom achievement at all levels.

Surely, the only disability in life is a bad attitude.

Looking back, my favorite teachers took responsibility for their own happiness, especially when they dropped it at the door and entered the classroom. And looking back further, I figured that they were about as happy as they made their minds up to be.

And looking back even more, my favorite teachers were resilient in the face of pessimism because they wanted to make our class the best place to be.

They Were Selfless

I don't know who said it, but one of my former students once gave me this quote: "When a man loves, he seeks no power. Therefore, he has power." As educators we can change that to "when a teacher loves, they seek no power. Therefore, they have power."

Selfless teachers are truly humble. The great Chinese philosopher Lao Tzu understood the paradoxical balance of humility and effective leadership. You know, it truly is a paradox. By being selfless, my favorite teachers naturally enhanced themselves. Of course, this was not done in a selfish way, but in a genuine, generous way. And yet another paradox: the more they gave away, the more they had.

In my opinion, absolutely nothing is gained by being a selfish educator. It creates a fearful, resentful, and greedy environment. How do I know this to be true?

Like many of my colleagues, I too tried to be selfish.

It didn't work.

I soon found out that if we smack out at the world, it naturally smacks us in return.

In retrospect, my selfishness only sparked more fires of displeasure, disagreement, and downright cynicism. Just like crabs in a bucket, when one crab wishes to crawl out and become free, the other crabs will pull the sojourner back into the petty mess of fear, suspicion, and greed. The crabs who wish to stay in the bucket and wallow in their unhappiness, see themselves as incomplete beings—beings who thrive on pessimism, despair, and gloom. I once heard a favorite teacher say that "bitchy people come in cycles." Although this statement can be a little harsh for the school environment, it does relate to the belief that incomplete teachers will attempt to make others incomplete as well. Fellow teachers, administrators, parents, or students—it doesn't matter who; the incomplete are out to increase their enrollment.

Therefore, I'll never forget the one-liner, "Bitchy people come in cycles." I'll never forget it because it reminds me that their behavior is not welcomed in the best place to be.

They Were Simple

They kept it simple. My favorite teachers could clear the clutter of the American popular culture like no other. They had a way of looking at clutter not only as garbage, but as emptiness. They could clear the emptiness of life with the waving of their hands. More importantly, they could clear the clutter of a confusing subject by simplifying it down to its very core. Let's face it, they could explain the subject well. They provided a basic foundation that supported us in growing individually with the subject matter being used as only an underpinning, not complete directions to all of life's answers.

They also understood "Wig Time."

The mind-style guru Anthony Gregorc introduced me to the term "Wig Time." Wig Time is the current, flashy, trendy, new thing in education, whatever it may be. Obviously, it must be the best choice, because it's a new wig. After all, it's Wig Time.

My favorite teachers were always open, but at the same time they understood the dangers of Wig Time. They understood the importance of age-old wisdom, humility, authenticity, and simplicity.

For example, one of my favorite teachers once told me that every complex and seemingly unsolvable disagreement, always starts out tiny and simple. The key to avoiding multifaceted problems was to address it while it was still undersized and manageable. Simplicity permeates the best place to be.

They Practiced Unconditional Love and Respect

One of my favorite teachers (trust guru Dennis McLoughlin) once told me at a workshop that "Jesus Christ hung out with people many Christians despise."

Whoa!

Since the topic was unconditional love and respect for all students, this quote has stayed with me ever since. In my earlier days of teaching, I never practiced unconditional respect for my students. After all, we had work to do. You know the type of work—tons of notes with nothing more, but more of the same. On top of all of this spectacular knowledge that I was dispensing, how could I possibly fit in the time for unconditional respect for my students? Well, sometimes I did. But looking back, it was more like compartmentalized unconditional respect. I showed love and respect only to those students who met my particular conditions.

My favorite teachers, however, showed genuine unconditional love and respect for all of their students. They loved their students because they were breathing and had heartbeats. And that was the only requirement for the best place to be.

They Were Criticized by Some

They were criticized by some, but not by most. My favorite teachers were respected by most and criticized by a few. But looking back, the few tended to be unhappy types who seemed to always blame someone or something for all of their problems. Dennis McLoughlin calls these unhappy educators, controllers. And believe me, I've been around many controllers. In fact, I used to be quite an all-star controller myself. As controlling educators, we never took full responsibility for our own choices. We were the type of teachers who demanded that students conform to and obey our petty rules and requirements. And if the student refused? Well, we would withdraw our respect and support from them.

The controlling teacher would especially criticize those colleagues who tried to reach out to all students. My favorite teachers were trusting educators who had dreams of hope and promise for all of their students. Trust psychologist McLoughlin gives teachers answers if things are going wrong in the classroom. He states all solutions in the form of a question and one goes like this: "You have a dream, an unrealistic one, that some people, if only they knew, would criticize you for having, don't you?"

This is my favorite educational quote and is one of the reasons that teaching is important to me. Those teachers that had a passion for the profession were criticized by some, but not by most.

Most importantly, they had dreams of someday influencing students toward their own autonomy, and it all started in the best place to be.

Finding the Passion in the Special Moments

Rena Faye Norby, Ph.D.

When I think about the joy and passion I've experienced in my years of teaching, I think of special moments that renew the energy and excitement I find in my teaching. I believe the decision to become a teacher comes from many different parts of our lives, our hearts, and our minds, but what stands out for me now are those particular times that have confirmed the rightness of my decision.

I came to teaching later than many teachers. I was twenty-nine years old when I realized how much fun it was to share something you had learned with other people in a classroom setting. At the time, I was a research scientist and a lab supervisor at the Georgia Tech School of Physics, and I had to teach a workshop for some people from the IBM research center in Fishkill, New York. What a special thrill it was for me when I realized the people whom I was teaching really wanted to hear what I had learned and could tell them about x-ray diffraction methods. Soon after this experience, I came to believe that I would enjoy teaching physics more than I enjoyed doing research in physics. I was still enthusiastic about learning science, but now I wanted to share that enthusiasm with others as a teacher. I applied to Georgia State University for the non-traditional teacher certification program, and to my delight I was accepted. With a little help from my sister-in-law, I was able to earn a M.Ed. degree in secondary science education. Much of my excitement and passion for teaching science was reinforced and expanded by the professors I had at Georgia State University. I was fortunate to attend at a time when there were five professors in the science education group. The humanistic science education movement had blossomed in that group in 1971. We students benefited from people who understood Piaget, Bruner, and Ausubel, and not only modeled how to teach in an active learning classroom, but welcomed us to the profession by taking us to science teacher meetings, having us in their homes as colleagues, and taking us on exceptional field experiences to schools in the Atlanta area and on field trips to the Georgia coast to study marine science teaching. Millie Graham, Jack Hassard, and Ed Lucy had all studied science education at Ohio State University and brought the quality and accomplishments of their experiences there to the classes they shared with me at Georgia State. Sometimes science education people from other schools called us the "weeds and beads" group. A lot of laughter and affirmation came out of that characterization; in retrospect, I know we were in the forefront of quantitative research in science education and were not just out there playing with the weeds when we were using square plots of fields to teach sampling methods and observation and reporting processes in science.

Much of my joy and inspiration in the lifelong profession and teaching has come from finding a community of like-minded professionals. Teachers have a combination of focus

and drive that is required for our profession, but also an elfin
spirit that makes us laugh when others might cry, find the
"teachable moment" in the most challenging of classroom
situations, and a cultivated yet inherent ability to create
lessons and classroom experiences that guide our students to
learning and becoming lifelong learners. Those professors at
Georgia State University helped me start my journey as a
member of our profession, and I still remember them with
gratitude and affection.

After my time at Georgia State, and some challenging
experiences teaching science with inner-city students who
were not able to read, I found a job teaching physics and
chemistry at a high school north of Atlanta. On my first day
of full-time high school teaching, a student came into my
class and announced that she would "never be a teacher." At
the time I smiled at her, and perhaps I thought about
responding, but I couldn't think of anything clever or even
illuminating to say, so I just smiled. Perhaps I even thought
that education would help to change her attitude toward our
profession. Later that fall, we had a chemistry lab where I
made a point to caution the students to be careful about using
Silver Nitrate, as it makes the skin black. After the lab, I
realized this same student had painted her entire palm with
the Silver Nitrate so that all of if was black! I learned
something that day about how our students challenge us,
sometimes in indirect and even bizarre ways. I have always
thought about this student and smiled because she taught me
that students will say and do many different things, at the
same time that they are letting us know they crave guidance
and perspective. As I recall, this student did fairly well in the
class. And in retrospect, the fact that she chose to sit at the

front of the class was an indication of how very interested she was in what went on in that class.

Often instructors tell their teacher-education students that we learn from our students during the first year of class. I am sure I learned a lot from my high school science students that first year, but I hope that I also provided some perseverance and even some humor for those young people.

During that first year, I had a sixth period chemistry class that wasn't composed of higher achievers. They were a small group, with one young man who shone in class because he obviously studied and always knew the answers to the questions I asked. The rest of the class was a mixed bunch—two young ladies who wanted to spend a lot of time in class combing their hair, two brothers who seemed to be very fond of me, but not so fond of studying chemistry. The group vindicated themselves, however, the day that the principal came to observe my class. The girls sat up straight and abstained from hair-combing that day, the rowdier class members were quiet and attentive, and, as I was reviewing for a test, the best student in the class answered the questions when no one else could pick up on the content thread.

Although that has been more than twenty-five years ago, I still remember many of those students fondly and often wonder what they are doing now. I met one of my physics students in a home improvement store about fifteen years ago. He now owns his own construction business and has a wife and a child. On the rare occasion when he wasn't in class, I am very glad I didn't turn him in for "skipping." I just knew there was a valid reason why he wasn't in class. Later on I found out that he'd had a sad family situation and that's why he wasn't in class.

How can I remember all these special and unique people after all this time? Perhaps because I came to teaching late and quit a career that would have been more rewarding in terms of money, but these young people at that high school validated my decision. In their own ways, they let me know that my methods, however unpolished and naive, were received with kindly attention and understanding. The small practical jokes they played on me still make me chuckle. The day that I took my earth science class on a field trip to Mt. Arabia, when it turned cold and we all thought we were going to freeze to death, is just another wonderful memory of how these supposedly cold, sophisticated teenagers were champs at rising to a difficult occasion and working at the learning goals I'd set for the trip!

My first high school physics class was a study in a bipolar achievement distribution, with no average students. Even before we were promoting cooperative learning group experiences in school, I'd divided that class into groups because I had no average students to teach to, just high achievers and below average achievers. Now I know how lucky I was that these kids had been in school together since first grade, so the people who were quick to learn the material didn't mind spending time with the students who took longer. Everyone learned—some from teaching their friends, and some from having other teachers as well as me. Word that I wasn't a bad physics teacher must have spread; the second year there were three first year physics classes when there had only been one class the first year. I had those students doing lab experiments in the hall with a twenty-five foot "slinky" because there wasn't room to measure the wavelengths in the classroom. My professors at Georgia State

University had convinced me that the best way to learn physics was hands-on, and I tried to make as many of the learning experiences hands on as I could. I'd turned in a lesson plan in the fall to have a lab in the parking lot in the spring, so the physics students could shoot water rockets to learn about forces of gravity and about how to measure the height of the rockets with a homemade quadrant. So when the principal decided to ban outside classes that spring, I'd already made a rationale for my lab, and he, somewhat grudgingly, I suspect, allowed us to do the lab in the parking lot. Some of the passion I still feel for teaching comes from that first year, when I tried out some of my new ideas and used some of those that my mentors had provided. I discovered the reward, the excitement, the absolute feeling of rightness that comes when you complete a lesson you've created, and it all comes together even better than you could have imagined. The exhilaration, the feeling of doing something for which you have a talent and a motivation, is almost inexpressible. However, if you are around a group of teachers for any length of time—whether they are in Spearfish, South Dakota, Atlanta, Georgia, or even Saratov, Russia—you will hear many times that infinite gusto of "I did it, and the students loved it."

When I had the privilege of being a Fulbright lecturer in Saratov, Russia (a city on the Volga River about 400 miles south of Moscow), I found that the educators and future educators I met there had that same spark of inspiration and dedication. These ardent people find ways to teach with limited resources, sometimes not knowing where their assigned classroom will be on any given day, and yet taking their students' needs into account and finding a way to serve those needs. I had an experience one day at the Saratov Pedagogical Institute that I can never forget or perhaps even equal. The teachers of English as a foreign language use music as one of their methods to help their students practice and become fluent in the language (with a British accent, up until now. After my time there, I believe there will be some speakers of English who will show a bit of a Southern accent.). I was invited to participate in assessing a group of second-year college students who were in Svetlana's class, and they sang, in unison, the Eagles' "Hotel California." My feelings and thoughts on this occasion were too many to describe in detail. But, suffice it to say, the joy and passion of the profession and rewards of teaching were never more alive in me than when I was with these young people while they demonstrated their learning. Svetlana served as my translator in my first weeks in Saratov and helped me learn how to travel on the "trolley-buses" that are a staple for transportation in this city of 800,000 souls. If I had not had the courage and passion to choose the profession that brought my passion and enthusiasm into focus, I would never have had the courage or the opportunity to make that trip to Russia and find a connection with fellow educators much like my friends here in the United States. I like to think my Russian students got to know an American educator with passion and dedication to our unique profession.

Not only do we as individual teachers have an irreplaceable experience when the design is implemented and the lesson clicks, but we also have the community of other teachers who share this feeling of rightness and who value the unique profession where we connect with our students not only as scholars and learners, but as providers of stimulus and emotional approval that fires our students to go into the adult world and use their intellects and passions to contribute to humankind. When our students leave our classrooms for the last time, we may not see them again. However, we know that we have planted a seed in their minds and hearts that may not sprout for many years. Like the Ponderosa pine seeds in Yellowstone National Park, it takes a fire to open the covering on that seed, and only when the special time comes and when the seed is needed does it find its mission. I know from my own experiences that is when we say, "Now I know what my sixth-grade teacher, Mr. Pounds, meant when he said 'Rena has never begun to extend herself." The seeds he planted in that classroom have continued to grow and flower for many years now. The only way I know to thank him is to do my very best to give that gift to my students.

Final Thoughts

There's an old joke about how teachers keep making you do something over and over until you get it right. This aphorism says something very central about our attitudes and habits as teachers. We have the patience with our students to let them keep practicing until they master what we're teaching. And we have the commitment and belief in the student that she or he will be able to achieve what we want to happen in the learning experience—to acquire more knowledge and to develop more processes of learning. Society seems to want to push teachers to do more in the areas of testing and reporting assessment because teachers are perceived to be so powerful in students' lives. I often tell my students that we receive more work because we've made teaching look so easy. Members of our society sit in school classrooms for twelve years or more. They apparently come to the belief that teachers are just "loafing along" because teachers organize their time and their classroom responsibilities so well that it looks pretty seamless to the consumers. Those people who say that teachers are in the profession for "June, July, and August" have little concept of how much time teachers spend throughout the year in planning; upgrading their skills; and making sure their lessons fit local, state, and national criteria. Much of my passion has come from the work that my teachers did for me when I was a public school student and from observing the dedication and productivity of today's teachers in the face of more complicated requirements than ever. There's no place where you will see harder working or more accomplished people than in a public school.

People come out of this system with literacy; education for becoming an informed member of society; skills in working with their fellow members of society in businesses, politics, and religion; and the capability of meeting the challenges of a complicated, scary world. These people are a testimonial to the special talents of professionals in teaching. How can I not find joy and passion in this? It has shaped my life and given me so many gifts that continue to challenge and reward me as an educator and as a human being.